Comrades

Comrades

Tales of a Brigadista

in the Spanish Civil War

Harry Fisher

University of Nebraska Press
Lincoln and London

Publication of this volume
was assisted by
The Virginia Faulkner Fund,
established in memory of Virginia Faulkner,
editor-in-chief of the
University of Nebraska Press.
First published 1998
by the University of
Nebraska Press
⊗ The paper in this book
meets the minimum
requirements of
American National Standard
for Information Sciences—
Permanence of Paper for
Printed Library Materials,
ANSI Z39.48-1984.
Library of Congress
Cataloging-in-Publication Data
Fisher, Harry, 1911–
Comrades : tales of a brigadista in
the Spanish Civil War / Harry Fisher.
p. cm.
Includes bibliographical references
(p. –) and index.
ISBN 0-8032-2006-5 (cl : alk. paper)
1. Fisher, Harry, 1911– . 2. Spain—
History—Civil War, 1936–1939—Personal
narratives, American. 3. Spain. Ejército
Popular de la República. Brigada
Internacional, XV—Biography. 4. Soldiers—
Spain—Biography. 5. Americans—Spain—
Biography.
I. Title.
DP269.A46F58 1998
946.081'8—dc21
98-4953
CIP

SECOND PRINTING: 1998

Contents

List of Illustrations

List of Illustrations

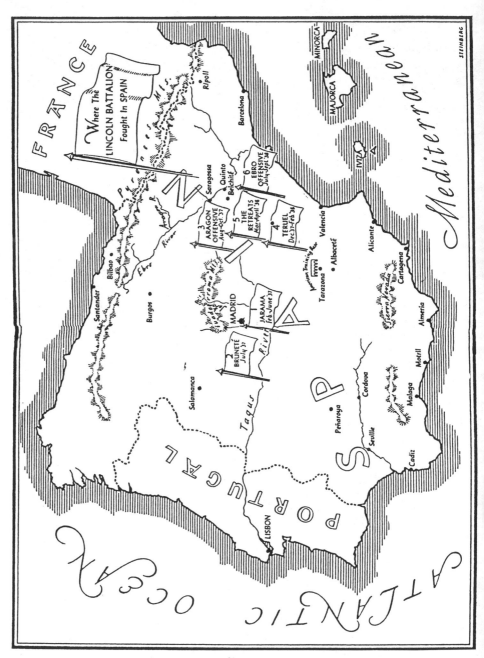

Where the Lincoln Battalion Fought in Spain.
Reprinted with permission of Mary Rolfe.

Foreword

THE SPANISH CIVIL WAR ended in 1939, but it will go down in history as the first battle of World War II. This book gives a close-up view of that battle. Beware starting to read it—you won't be able to put it down. It is an honest, well-written autobiographical account of the time sixty years ago when Harry Fisher was a member of the Abraham Lincoln Brigade, a group of Americans who volunteered to fight fascism years before it was popular to do so. I am so glad he has written this story. It will hold you from beginning to end.

In 1937 I was eighteen, a counselor at a summer camp, when the carpentry teacher suddenly quit in midsummer. Months later I found out he'd gone to Spain. The three thousand American Brigadistas became part of the forty-thousand-strong International Brigades. They were communists, socialists, anarchists, and unaffiliated heroes from fifty countries who volunteered to help defend the elected government of Spain when it was attacked by General Francisco Franco. Franco was aided by planes, tanks, men, and materiel supplied by Hitler and Mussolini, and while the government of the United States, along with those of France and England, officially declared neutrality, American corporations such as Texaco also helped Franco by sending him much-needed oil via Italy. After two and a half years of slaughter, Franco won.

Now historical evidence bears out that it was the policy of England, France, and some sectors of the United States to build up Hitler and Mussolini, hoping they'd attack the Soviet Union. And in the sense that history has exposed these truths that were not recognized sixty years ago, the Brigadistas have won.

In the late 1930s I began to learn some of the songs those heroic young people sang as they tried to stop European fascism. I still sing "Viva la Quince Brigada, Rhumbala, Rhumbala" for young audiences who, along with a large majority of the world's 6 billion people, realize that ridding the planet of weapons of war will be a major job of the twenty-first century.

The heroism of the International Brigades will stand for all time. It's one world or no world. ¡Viva la Quince Brigada!

Pete Seeger
June 1997

Preface

TODAY, MOST AMERICANS, especially the young, know about the Spanish Civil War only through works of fiction such as Ernest Hemingway's *For Whom the Bell Tolls*. Sadly, the real stories of those who were there are not being handed down to new generations. These stories may well be lost to history, a significant loss as there are meaningful lessons to be learned from them, and message-bearing voices to be heard. But most of the men and women who went to Spain in the late 1930s to help the Spanish people put an end to fascism are nameless, faceless, forgotten.

I wrote this book for several reasons. At first, I thought of it as a letter of sorts, written for family and close friends as a way of explaining why I went to Spain in 1937. Later, I came to feel a profound need to remember and honor my comrades, particularly those who sought no glory and received none, but who also received no recognition or even mention in history books. I still see their youthful faces in my dreams at night and in my daydreams as well, as clear to me now as they were sixty years ago. It's impossible to erase their images from my mind.

It angers me that countless U.S. administrations have treated us like pariahs, President Reagan even commenting once that the Lincolns fought on the wrong side in the Spanish Civil War! The three thousand Americans who joined forty thousand other Internationals to try to stop fascism before it could gain a foothold in Europe were pegged "premature anti-fascists" by the Roosevelt administration, which had, along with the other democracies, refused to acknowledge the threat posed by Hitler and Mussolini until Spain had been decimated. And so anger played a part in my writing this book.

Most of my stories concern the men I lived, worked, and fought side by side with for nineteen months. I would have liked to write about the equally idealistic women who participated in this anti-fascist struggle. But most of them were nurses, and because, fortunately for me, I was never wounded, I did not come into direct contact with them. I do have tremendous respect for them to this day, having heard the stories told by my comrades of their courage and selflessness.

Another reason for writing this book was that I wanted to reiterate a sentiment expressed by some—but not enough—"soldier-writers" before me. War is never glorious; it is never an adventure. War is truly a taste of hell. There could not have been a more justifiable cause than ours in Spain. But even in its most honorable form, war is still a horror that brings to humankind nothing but misery. And so I am left with a puzzling question. Which is the greater evil: fascism or war? The answer for me was and is fascism. This is not to say that war is an acceptable solution to the problem presented by fascism. Perhaps in 1937 it was the only solution. Today there is a great need to instill in our youth a hatred for war and a desire to find peaceful solutions to the evils brought on society by bigots and bullies. I hope that this book about war will be thought of as one that carries strictly an antiwar message.

As I write these words, there are only about 150 Lincolns living, and many of them are ailing in nursing homes and hospitals. Believe it or not, some—well into their eighties now—are still actively fighting to make this a better country and a better world. I must thank all of them—the ninety-five percent who are not alive and the five percent who still are—for living their lives in harmony with their ideals, and in this way making this book possible.

Specifically, I want to thank the veterans who provided me with photos, letters, and stories: John Murra, Norman Berkowitz, Clarence Kailin, Jack Shafran, and Ralph Fasanella. Sam Walters invited me to browse through his superb collection of photos and to use anything I liked. I am very grateful, especially for his photo of Oliver Law leading the Lincolns in our attack at Villanueva de la Cañada: This is truly a remarkable photo. And my thanks to Mary Rolfe for giving me permission to use the best battle map of the Spanish Civil War.

I appreciate the kind words and suggestions of the few Lincolns who read the manuscript before publication—Bill Susman, Abe Smorodin, and Moe Fishman. Also gracias to Jack Karan for his encouragement and very helpful comments.

Some years ago, veteran Charles Nusser read an early version of the manuscript, the first person outside my family to do so. Though he died in 1993, I wish to give him heartfelt thanks for the poignant words he said to me, words that I remember to this day. He said that the manuscript made him relive the nightmare of the war and made him realize anew how important it is that we put an end to all such horrors. He said it was not a war story but an antiwar story. That was the finest compliment I could have received; his words moved me to finish and polish this work.

I cannot let this opportunity go by without thanking my good friends Lou and Edna Zucker for saving the letters I wrote to Lou from Spain, and for their insistence over the years that I write of my experiences.

Profound thanks go to Eunice Lipton for her enthusiasm regarding the manuscript and for putting me in touch with the good people at the University of Nebraska Press. Her friendship and support this past year have been very important to me. And thanks to Eunice's husband, Ken Aptekar, for coming up with the title for the book!

Thanks too to Professor Cary Nelson and Professor Jefferson Hendricks for their flattering comments and for their friendship.

Pete Seeger can never know how good his wonderful words that begin this book made me feel. He has always been one of my heroes, not only for his inspiring music but for his courage and steadfastness through years of political struggle.

Many thanks to Peggy Garry for her meticulous legal advice and assistance. She was of tremendous help.

And now I come to the members of my family who played such a major role in this project. First, my sister, Sal, who saved more than a hundred letters that I wrote to her and her family. It was through those letters that I was able to recall so many events and details from long ago. But the letters alone could not have prodded me to write this book. Through the years, it was my brother-in-law and sister-in-law, Zoltan and Fay Grad, who relentlessly urged me to write of my experiences . . . and finally succeeded. Also, my niece Louise and her husband, Milt Becker, have offered consistent support and enthusiasm for this project.

My son, John, was responsible for an important aspect of the book. It was he who got me to write about the negative incidents I witnessed during the war. About five years ago, I decided to tell him some stories that had tormented me for half a century, stories I had shared with practically no one. John listened, and when I was done he said quietly: "You must tell those stories in your book." I was shocked at this suggestion and told him that I couldn't, because critics would use them to discredit the International Brigades. The life-affirming work of the vast majority of the Internationals should not be smeared by a few renegades, I told him, and this is what I believed would happen if I related those distasteful stories. John insisted that my book must be honest, that leaving negative stories out would make it little more than propaganda. He insisted that I tell the whole story, the good and the bad, and that the good would surely shine through. I was not convinced.

Then I talked with my daughter, Wendy, and told her the ugly stories and what John had suggested. I was sure she would agree with me, that such things are best forgotten, but to my surprise she agreed with her brother and gave the same reasons he had given. It took some time for me to come around, but I finally did find myself agreeing with my children. I am grateful to both of them for helping me change my mind.

Wendy is the person who worked so diligently on the book these last few years. She showed no mercy in making me go over every detail until it was right and readable. It is impossible to thank her enough. I must also thank Geoffrey Ithen, my son-in-law, for all the effort he put into the book. He found many technical errors and also used his photography expertise to improve the condition of the very old photos that I wanted to include. Gracias Geoff. And gracias to Dena Fisher, my daughter-in-law, for all her encouragement over the years.

I come now to my last gracias, to my late wife Ruthie. In our early years together she deliberately avoided all discussion about the ugly experiences I had during the war. We talked about the humorous episodes only. I will never forget her understanding and compassion at that time in my life and in our fifty-four years of marriage.

When my sister, Sal, gave us the packet of letters she had saved from Spain, Ruthie read them all, some over and over again. When she was finished, she said, "Harry, someday you must write a book about this. It would be good to have it published, but even if it never is you must share these experiences with our friends and family. I want them to know that you were one of the three thousand Americans who tried to put an end to fascism before it was popular to do so." Ruthie knew and had a deep love for many of the American volunteers who went to Spain, and she wanted their stories to be heard as well.

Several months before her death, Ruthie told me that she would like to write a few words for the book, and as it turned out, they were the last words she ever wrote:

I awoke on September 21, 1938, to the sound of wind and rain beating against the window. One of the worst hurricanes ever to hit New York had struck overnight. As an organizer and business agent for Local 1250 of the Department Store Employees Union, one of my assignments was to greet members of our union returning from the civil war in Spain; eleven had gone. One, Harry Fisher, was scheduled to arrive that morning on the *Ile de France.*

At 9:00 A.M. I called Clarina Michelson, president of the union, to say that the weather was impossible, and I didn't know if I could make it to the pier. Clarina showed little sympathy and told me that if our boys could fight fascism in Spain, under all weather conditions, then surely some wind and rain should not stop me. "Get to that pier," she said, and she hung up.

Because Harry had left for Spain before I joined the staff of the union I had never met him and was uncertain how I would identify him. But when I arrived at the pier, I saw Harry's sister, Sal, who sometimes worked at the union office. She introduced me to their mother. I put my arm around his mother and marveled at her patience and stoicism.

The ship had already docked. My eyes had been glued to the gangplank for some time when at last I saw a particularly cute guy disembark. I watched as he walked rapidly, then almost ran toward us. It was Harry.

Harry and his mother hugged and kissed each other. She was

not quite so calm now and kept repeating, "Are you all right, are you all right?" Harry tried to assure her that he had not been wounded. Not satisfied, she checked his arms, hands, fingers, legs, even his ears. Then she sighed with great relief and was once again calm and composed. To my surprise, she gestured toward me and said to Harry, "Nu, kiss the maidl." I remember thinking how inappropriate this was; she should have said "Shake hands with your union organizer."

After asking Harry about our union members still in Spain waiting to come home, I left for the union office. Harry went home with his mother.

A few days later, Harry came to the union office, and I started on the next phase of my responsibility: finding jobs for the returning vets. Not an easy task in 1938. After a few more days, I succeeded in getting Harry a job at Norton's Department Store.

Many of the union's young women, and men as well, were eager to participate in the welcoming home celebrations. Every Saturday Harry came to the parties we organized to help the vets get back into circulation, but he usually left early. After the sixth or seventh party, Harry said to me, "No more parties. How about a date. Just me and you." We dated. Our mutual interests grew, our friendship deepened. We were in love, and we married in May of 1939.

Harry was still trying to overcome the bewilderment of his family and some friends about why he had gone to Spain. We began to think it might be a good idea to try to answer the family's questions in a more formal way, by putting something in writing. Sal had saved all of Harry's letters from Spain, which recounted his experiences in great detail but with little organization. We began the project of typing the stories, and putting them into a more structured format.

We worked on the project sporadically. When the Second World War began, Harry enlisted in the U.S. Army Air Force and flew twenty-two missions as an engineer-gunner aboard a B-26 bomber. Harry was once again involved in the fight against fascism.

After the war, children, jobs, McCarthyism, and crises of one sort or another caused further delays. Although the idea of a book chronicling Harry's experiences in Spain never left us, it wasn't until recent years that we were able to resume work on, and finally finish, the project.

The question "Why did you go to Spain?" is still asked, now by a new generation unfamiliar with the depth and consequences of the Great Depression and of the devastating effects of fascism. Today, as the world becomes frighteningly reminiscent of the 1930s, a new and wider audience may find the experiences of an earlier generation interesting and enlightening.

Ruth Fisher
New York City, 1993

Introduction

"We fought to make Madrid the tomb of fascism."
——La Pasionaria

DURING THE 1930S the United States suffered its severest depression. It was a time of deep anguish for millions of unemployed Americans; it was also a time of widespread political activity. During this period the New Deal was developed, the Congress of Industrial Organization (CIO) was formed, and American radicalism grew into a strong and influential force. The decade of the thirties saw union organizing, massive strikes, demonstrations by the unemployed, hunger marches, and veterans' bonus marches.

Throughout the world, this decade was a time of social, political, and economic upheaval.

Adolf Hitler began his reign of terror in 1933, when the German Reichstag placed absolute power in his hands. Berlin became the center of fascism, a racist ideology, brutal and arrogant, with visions of world domination.

In July 1936, the Spanish fascist Falange led sections of the armed forces of Spain into open rebellion against the popularly elected government of the Spanish Republic. A wave of anger and fear swept over the world. The "Rome-Berlin Axis," the governments of fascist Italy and Nazi Germany, plotted the rebellion of General Francisco Franco and supplied massive armament and material aid to the rebel forces. The conquest of Spain was to be a milestone on the road to world domination.

Compassion and sympathy were felt around the world for the Spanish people and for the democratic government that only recently had deposed a centuries-old monarchy, instituted land reforms, built schools and hospitals, and begun to bridge the gap between feudalism and democracy. Forty thousand men and women, including three thousand Americans, came from all corners of the earth to fight alongside the Spanish people.

In 1937 I was one of eleven members of the Department Store Employees Union, Local 1250, who went to Spain. The others were Norman Berkowitz, Irving Chocheles, Gerald ("Jerry") Cook, Bernard ("Butch") Entin, Irving ("Toots") Fajans, Hy Roseman, William Schultz, Jack Shafran, Leon Tenor, and Morton Wolson. I suppose it could be said that as a group we were lucky. Fully one third of the Americans who fought in Spain never came home; only two in our group, Butch Entin and Bill Schultz, died there. Six of our number were wounded, and one was captured and held as a prisoner of war for over a year. Irv Chocheles and I were the only two in our group to escape injury or capture.

The events in which we had participated at home had had a direct influence on our decisions to go to Spain. We were trade unionists. We had worked with the unemployed and the poor. In many ways, we viewed the Spanish struggle as an extension of our fight against reaction at home. Most significantly, we wanted to focus the nation's attention on the growing threat of fascism, and the danger it posed to international peace. We were later to be called "premature anti-fascists," and we accepted this title proudly, though it was not meant as a compliment by the State Department spokesman who first coined the term. After all, we had bucked the system—the U.S. government, even under Franklin Delano Roosevelt, had remained neutral in the various worldwide struggles against fascism, right up until the time World War II began. But in 1937 many people around the world did recognize the threat fascism brought to world peace, and it was our fervent hope that by aborting the fascist takeover in Spain, we might prevent a second world war.

1. The Great Depression

IN 1929 I WAS WORKING in the New York office of the Henry Rose Stores, the women's wear division of Sears Roebuck, earning fifteen dollars for a forty-eight-hour week. The first thing I remember after getting the job was the big stock market crash of October 29. "Black Thursday," as that fateful day was known, brought with it chaos and the end of America's eight years of prosperity—an economic boom that had made the rich richer and the poor all but invisible.

A couple of days after the crash, my boss gave me a note to bring to the Bank of the U.S. His friend, the bank's vice president, had told him that the bank would close down the following day. When I got there, I saw a long line of anxious people outside, all waiting to get into the bank to withdraw their savings. Many policemen were stationed there, and were allowing only a few people in at a time. I showed my note to the bank official standing at the entrance. He admitted me right away. I found the vice president and gave him the note. He immediately gave me a bank check for $50,000 with instructions to deposit it in another bank. I went right to that bank and made the deposit. Later that day I felt guilty when I remembered the worried faces of those poor people who couldn't get into the bank to save their few hard-earned dollars, while my millionaire boss had no trouble rescuing his money.

That night, when I got home, I found my mother in tears. For twenty years she had worked in a garment factory under sweatshop conditions and had managed to save about $1,500, which she kept in the Bank of the U.S. Now it was gone. She was inconsolable.

About two months after the bank closing, another incident shook me. I was still at the Henry Rose Stores; it was Saturday at noon, the end of the work week, and we had just gotten our pay envelopes. As I was putting on my coat, I heard cries coming from the women's locker room. I went in and asked what had happened. One of the women told me that about fifty of them had gotten pink slips in their envelopes. That was it. There was no two-week notice, no severance pay, just a pink slip saying they were not needed anymore. Many of these young women came from families in which they were the only ones working, and it would be impossible for them to get any other job now that the Depression had hit. Factories, offices, and stores were closing all over the country. At that time there was no unemployment insurance, so if no one in the family was working, it meant hunger and despair.

During the early Depression years, it was common to see families evicted from their apartments, their furniture on the sidewalk in front of the slum tenements, and the families standing guard over their few worldly possessions. Often the children, the mother, and sometimes the father too, would be on the sidewalk, not knowing what to do. One day I was amazed to see a group of young people carrying furniture back to an apartment from which a family had been evicted. One young woman gave leaflets to passersby explaining what they were doing. When I saw that the organization responsible for carrying the furniture back up five flights was the Young Communist League, it was enough to make me join up. It made me feel good to know there was an organization that didn't just talk, but actually did something. For months afterward, I participated with other YCLers in carrying furniture up two, three, four, and even five flights. It was backbreaking work for me, because I weighed only about 115 pounds. But the work was fairly distributed, with the huskier men carrying the heavier furniture, while smaller fellows carried the lighter stuff.

Police were always on the streets when the evictions took place, but they rarely interfered with us when we were returning the furniture to the apartment. They simply turned their backs and looked away. They also felt sympathy for these people. Even the sheriffs who organized the evictions and carried the furniture out to the street didn't mind our carrying the furniture back. They were paid by the landlord to carry out the eviction, but not to enforce it, so if the furniture went back, they had to repeat the eviction, and for that they received more money. In some cases, when it was raining, we didn't wait for the sheriff to leave the area. We immediately began to carry the furniture back. The sheriff would smile and leave; he knew he would be back. Some landlords stopped evicting tenants, because it proved to be too expensive.[1]

In autumn 1932 I attended Commonwealth College in Arkansas's Ozark Mountains. This was a small, radical, labor college, with students from all over the country. I remember one assignment for which I had to interview farmers in the area surrounding the college. These farmers lived in one of the most isolated and undeveloped sections of the country. In the area I visited, there were no paved roads, just some very narrow, bumpy paths, obviously meant for horse-and-wagon use. But many of these farmers didn't even own a horse. I discovered that some of them had never been more than a few miles from their homes. This part of the Ozark Mountains was their world.

And were they poor! I was aghast at what I saw. I remember going to one farmhouse after another; most of the shacks had only one room, no running water, no electricity, no indoor toilets. Some farmers didn't even have outhouses and had to use ditches for toilets. I always thought that there was plenty to eat on farms, so I was shocked to see the farmers and their families so thin and bony. They all wore rags for clothing and were shoeless. The children went to school only two months out of the year; the farmers themselves were semiliterate. There was one thing that practically every shack had in common: a huge beach umbrella over the bed, with a hole in the center of the bed to hold the pole. I asked one farmer why the umbrellas were there, and he explained, "When the heavy rains come, the roof leaks, and this keeps the bed dry."

One farmer I interviewed blamed his poverty, his misery, and all his problems on the "Wall Street Jews." I asked him, "Which Wall Street Jews are you talking about?" "Rockefeller," he answered.

In that area, discrimination against blacks was so strong that blacks were forbidden by law to stay in town after dark. One of the students' aims at Commonwealth was to break this barrier. We planned to have blacks join the student body and to invite Paul Robeson to lecture. We would introduce Robeson as a great American scholar, singer, athlete, and actor, and we would invite all the neighboring farmers to attend the event. Unfortunately, the faculty opposed our program, so we set up a picket line, which brought on the sheriff and his men, armed with shotguns.

Next thing we knew we'd been expelled. So, in December, those of us who were expelled left Commonwealth College and headed for Chicago. The women piled into two old beat-up cars, and the rest of us went by freight. It was my first experience riding the rails. We rode on the outside of a tanker, standing on a narrow walk-around and holding on to a rail that encircled the tanker. It was bitter cold, snowing, and as the train went speeding along at sixty miles an hour, the snow hit our faces like needles. Soon I began to feel warm and sleepy. I called over to the person standing next to me and told him how good I felt. He became agitated and warned me that feeling warm and sleepy was dangerous and meant that I could freeze to death. He urged me to jump up and down on the railing, and he put his arm around me to make sure I didn't fall off.

Luckily the train soon made a stop at Kansas City. I don't know if I could have lasted much longer. After a few days, we took another freight train to Chicago. This time we all went into a boxcar where the cold was intense, but not as bad as staying on the outside of the tanker during a snowstorm. There were about twenty-five of us from Commonwealth, and quite a few others, jammed into that boxcar.

In Chicago, we searched for work, participated in unemployment demonstrations, and attended an antiwar congress at the University of Chicago at Christmastime, as evidenced by the following letter that I wrote to my friend Nat Lieber. In it I talk about this congress, as well as meetings with Jane Addams, the tireless activist and founder of Hull House who had recently won the Nobel Peace Prize.

December 28, 1932
Dear Nat:

I meant to write to you during the holidays, but I never found the time to do so. It happens that I am the only one in the apartment just now and I have only a few moments to write a few words. The rest of the crowd are over at the University of Chicago attending the anti-war congress. . . . A bunch of New Yorkers came in last night to attend. . . .

There are lots of things happening concerning the strike these days. We had dinner at the Hull House the other day with Jane Addams for the second time. She is trying to settle things up with the association and the striking students so that schools like Commonwealth won't suffer from the resulting bad name it gets as a result of this strike. There is an agreement now, at least on our part, that there will be some sort of arbitration to settle the differences between the association and the strikers. Jane Addams has written to the school to see whether they will accept sending representatives to the association in this dispute. There is no doubt that the association will accept, not that they want to, but because they feel that Jane Addams will not help support them by contributions unless they show up for this trial. The arbitration committee will consist of three men, one to be chosen by us, one by the association and the third to be chosen by those two. We have already chosen Scott Nearing who is now at the anti-war congress. . .

Despite our best efforts, Commonwealth College was not to survive. Some years later, local farmers burned the building to the ground.[2]

Shortly after the antiwar congress ended, I made my way back to New York. I had been away from home for only a few months, but I was astonished to see the long bread lines. For hours, thousands of men and women would wait in line for a bowl of soup and a piece of bread. There were Hoovervilles all over the city, in empty lots in residential neighborhoods, and sometimes in the parks.

I was broke when I returned from Chicago, and I needed to find a job. I spent days walking up and down Sixth Avenue, going in and out of employment agencies. Crowds of people gathered in front of each agency reading the notices for nonexistent jobs that were pasted on the windows. I filed forms in agency after agency, day after day, week after week, for many months. Some jobs were available for dishwashers in restaurants, where you received your meals in exchange for your labor, but no money. Once I was offered a job that included a salary. The job was working in the steam room of a laundry that was in Brooklyn, about a half-mile from the last subway stop. The pay was twelve dollars a week, and the hours were from eight in the morning until seven at night, Monday through Saturday. My job was to open huge machines and throw the dirty laundry into the boiling, steaming water. The room was unbearably hot, with the temperature easily over a hundred degrees. After one hour I was ready to pass out, so I quit.

On the subway ride back to Manhattan, my thoughts went to my father, who had died at the age of twenty-eight, when I was three years old. I remembered the stories my mother told us of the long hours he worked in a steamy sweatshop in the garment industry. Before long he became ill with tuberculosis, was hospitalized, and died a few years later.

In 1934 the bathrobe workers, members of the Trade Union Unity League, were on strike. One day they asked our YCL branch for help on the picket line.

At 7:30 the next morning about twenty YCLers showed up at the picket line. The striking workers were mostly middle-aged and elderly women. It was peaceful enough, with ten policemen standing by, quietly watching us, until eight o'clock, when a number of cars pulled up in front of the building. Immediately the police parted the picket line and made a path for the scabs to go through. One elderly woman shouted: "Don't let the scabs in!"

Unfortunately we didn't have enough people there to stop them. A few of us, some strikers and some YCLers, did manage to get close to the entrance, and we all shouted to the scabs not to go in. Then, suddenly, a grim, tough, husky man pushed his face near mine and grunted: "Beat it, kid, or you're dead." I looked down and saw a pistol pressing into my stomach. I was so surprised that I didn't have time to be frightened. I yelled to a nearby policeman: "Officer, this man has a gun in my stomach!"

The policeman quickly came to my side, looked down at the gun, grabbed me by the shoulder, and said: "You're under arrest!" I protested indignantly: "He's got the gun! Why are you arresting me?"

The cop pulled me around the corner and said, "What the hell's the matter with you, kid? That man's a gangster. Beat it before you get shot!"

A few months later, still unable to get a job and dead broke, I decided to ride the freights and look for a job elsewhere, along with a friend from Commonwealth College, Hugo Fischer. So, without a penny in our pockets, we got a ride to New Jersey and from there caught a freight train to Washington. When we got to DC the next morning we were starved, so we went to the Salvation Army for breakfast. There were about two hundred people crowded into a small hall, sitting on benches and just waiting. There were men and women, though mostly men, of all ages, from sixteen to over eighty. A few seemed to be professional hoboes, but most of the people were just like us—jobless and penniless. The minister informed us that he would like us to sing some hymns before we had breakfast. We sang sadly, and without enthusiasm. He asked us to please put some spirit into our voices, and he assured us that breakfast was waiting. We shouted at the top of our lungs; we shook the rafters, and then we waited eagerly for food. We were given a bowl of cold, thick oatmeal, stale bread, and coffee. It tasted good.

Then we visited a friend of Hugo's, Lem Harris, at the office of the National Farmers Union. Harris asked us if we could go to Wisconsin to cover the farm strike that was going on there. The National Farmers Union had a monthly newspaper but did not have a correspondent in Wisconsin. We accepted and became the correspondents for the Farmers Union even though we knew nothing about farming. (I figured that was OK, because some of the daily newspapers had reporters covering factory strikes, even though they had never worked in a factory.) That evening we jumped a freight again and were on our way. I was appalled at how many people were on these freight trains. Most of the men were traveling from city to city looking for work. Some were men looking for work so they could send money back to their families. In some cases, the men had their wives and children with them, because they had no home to stay in. I remember one family with a little baby.

They were all very helpful to us and warned us what to expect. They told us to get off the train when it stopped in the evening, and that we should expect to be pulled in by the local police. And that is exactly what happened. We were all carted off to jail where we got something to eat and slept on a cold cement floor with mice and roaches all over the place. We were not actually arrested, however. The police just wanted to keep us off the streets for the night and to make sure that we got out of town in the morning. And sure enough, a little after dawn, the police escorted all the jailbirds to the freight yards and waited for us to get on a freight and out of their town.

We arrived in West Allis, Wisconsin, only to learn that the strike was over and that a victory celebration was already in progress. Hugo and I went over to the hall, where we—the "press"—were greeted warmly and enthusiastically by the jubilant farmers. Here I met a wonderful family, the Rodys, whose son John would later join me in Spain.

While we were at the victory celebration we learned that in about a week there was going to be a hunger march from all parts of Wisconsin to the state capital, Madison. Many organizations, including the Communist and Socialist parties, organizations for the unemployed, trade unions, and social organizations, participated in planning the march. Meetings were held in churches and settlement houses. The people were angry, militant, and anxious to do something about the hunger that was all around them in the richest dairy state in the country.

Hugo and I were invited to attend the meetings and to participate in the hunger march. We joined the marchers from Milwaukee and surrounding areas. This group consisted of more than three thousand people. The march to Madison was about one hundred miles, and the plan was for it to take four days.

I got to know the people of this area during those four days. I was asked, along with three others, to be on a committee to collect food for the marchers. Our job was to go ahead of the crowd, stop at farmhouses, and ask for food for the hunger marchers. We received a warm reception from the farmers along the route. We expected sympathy from the poor farmers, but the generosity from both poor and rich farmers was terrific. We didn't have to talk much about the purpose of the march, because the farmers had read about it in the newspapers and heard about it on the radio.

They piled sacks on the road filled with bread, hard-boiled eggs, and freshly harvested vegetables. I was better fed during the hunger march than I had been in years.

We walked most of the day, while the elderly, and those who fell ill, rode in cars and trucks. Our procession stretched out for miles. During the night we slept in churches and trade-union halls; some elderly people were taken into private homes.

One evening the local newspaper in the town where we were staying had a large, bold, scare headline: "KEEP THE REDS OUT." The article was about the American Legion and other patriotic organizations in a neighboring town arming their members with bats, clubs, and iron pipes to keep us from coming into their town.

After a quick meeting of the leaders of the march, a group of our American Legionnaires, veterans of World War I, wearing their legionnaire caps, got onto one of the trucks and sped there. When the local legionnaires saw that these marchers were also veterans, their whole attitude changed. They joined with the trade unions and churches to welcome and feed us. Many of our people, especially our vets, were given places to sleep in the American Legion hall, and others were invited to the homes of local vets. It turned out to be a grand evening, with entertainment, lots of beer, and even a speech by the mayor, who was also a veteran.

Finally we arrived in Madison. We were amazed to see that there were far more people than we had expected. We were hoping for ten thousand, but the Madison paper estimated that there were about twenty thousand.

The first night we camped out along a lake, not far from the University of Wisconsin. Many students joined us, as did a large group of American Indians from the northern part of Wisconsin. We stayed up all night going from one group to another, listening to discussions and singing songs. Food was plentiful. The trade unions, churches, Communist Party, Socialist Party, and American Legion supplied us with food, coffee, and beer.

The next morning we all marched to the capitol. Unfortunately the governor had to leave on "important business," and a few other politicians also disappeared. Some did stay to address the rally. It was very moving and impressive. And I remember thinking how broad the labor movement had become when I saw in Wisconsin the same slogan I had seen so many times in New York at demonstrations of the unemployed: "Don't Starve—Fight!"

And back once again in New York, the message was very much the same. In December of 1934, after attempts to negotiate contracts had failed, the workers at Ohrbach's and Klein's department stores went on strike. Local 1250 of the Department Store Employees Union called for assistance on the picket lines. My YCL branch was asked to help. Because I was unemployed at the time, I went down to the union and volunteered my services. It was then that I first met Leon Tenor, Irv Fajans, Jerry Cook, Jack Shafran, Irv Chocheles, Butch Entin, and Bobby Rice (son of the playwright Elmer Rice), as well as Clarina Hanks Michelson, the imaginative and charismatic leader of the union.

Born into a wealthy, conservative family in 1892, and related to Abraham Lincoln, Clarina left her life of privilege, as she often said, "to do something about the fact that a few people appeared to have most of the money, while the majority of people didn't have nearly enough." She became a union organizer and devoted her life to the labor movement. Somewhat older than the rest of us, she would regale us with stories from her past. She told us about working with coal miners in Harlan County, Kentucky. Once, while chairing a meeting, shots were fired into the meeting hall. Several men jumped up and hastily ran from the room. The meeting continued and Clarina tried to reassure the audience, asking them to be calm, and not to be as fearful as the men who had left. One of the miners, a tall, thin man, as Clarina described him, stood up to set Clarina straight: "Ma'am, them fellas ain't afraid; they just went home to get their guns."

Clarina also was a longtime friend of Gypsy Rose Lee, the well-known stripper with a social conscience. She would speak at union meetings—often the most well attended meetings we held.

During the Ohrbach's strike, the police allowed only three pickets on the line. We didn't make a big fuss about that during the week because the store wasn't that busy. But on Saturday, the busy day, we always tried to have mass picket lines to stop people from going into the store.

However, as soon as there were more than three pickets marching in front of the store, the mounted and foot policemen charged in.

I remember one Saturday morning, it was still very early, and I was one of the three pickets in front of Ohrbach's. Suddenly, I noticed a large group of people carrying picket signs coming down Fourteenth Street toward the store. I knew this must be our Saturday mass picket line. The group was led by Dorothy Day, editor of the *Catholic Worker*, and behind her were dozens of priests and nuns all carrying signs saying "God Supports the Poor," "God Supports the Strikers," "Jesus Is on the Side of the Strikers." The police, always ready to swing into action, paused when they saw this group. They seemed confused and looked toward their captain for guidance. He didn't know what to do. This was one Saturday when the picket line was not smashed.

Clarina also organized famous writers, artists, theater people, lawyers, and doctors to picket on Saturdays. Once, the members of the United Scenic Artists joined in. The picket line was very big, and the artists were very vocal and militant. Of course, we were all arrested. At the police station, instead of giving their own names the artists gave names such as Leonardo da Vinci, Michelangelo, and so on. Each time the desk sergeant would peer at the artist and groan. Then, Hugo Gellert, who was president of the union, came before the sergeant. Perhaps because he was the head of the union, he believed that he should give his right name, so he stated proudly that his name was Hugo Gellert. This time the sergeant threw down his pen and exploded: "I know that one's a phony!"

I remember another time when a Rolls Royce pulled up in front of the store. Immediately the police rushed over to make a path through the picket line for these obviously wealthy shoppers. One chauffeur opened the door for the two women inside; yet another chauffeur opened the trunk of the car—and out came picket signs asking the public to support the strikers. The two women, picket signs in hand, represented the League of Women Shoppers, they told us, and they walked the line with us, calling on bystanders to join us. The police were dumbfounded. One of the women was the wife of Arthur Garfield Hayes, one of the most prominent lawyers in the country, and head of the American Civil Liberties Union. The police did not interfere with that picket line either.

One person I got to know very well during the Ohrbach's strike was

Butch Entin. Not too tall, but sturdily built, he was a tough, yet gentle, loyal, and wise young man. He was one of the most militant members of the Department Store Union. He too had been arrested many times on the picket line, and we had spent time in jail together.

One night, after we were arrested on the Ohrbach's picket line, we were sitting in a cell, waiting for the judge to open the night-court session. Outside the cell was the arresting officer, in a bad humor because he was spending too many Saturday nights in court. Somehow, I got into an argument with him, and he threatened to beat the hell out of me. I taunted him, and he challenged me to meet him at Stillman's Gym. I agreed but never intended to do so, because he was at least sixty pounds heavier than I. But Butch, thinking I was getting myself into something I couldn't handle, came up to the front of the cell and said, "Hey, this kid can't fight, and besides, he's a lightweight. How about you and me meeting at the gym?" The cop eyed Butch for a moment, then backed off. "Aw, I was only kidding," the cop muttered as he walked away.[3]

Those were some days, the strikes, the clashes, the meetings, the discussions—and the togetherness. We talked about things that were happening all over the world, as well as the problems facing the union. We were concerned about Mussolini's attack on Ethiopia; we felt a deep anger about the unhindered rise of Hitler in Germany, and about our own Nazi sympathizers right here in America.

We talked about the bosses who were doing everything to smash the unions. They didn't hesitate to use gangsters and stool pigeons; they fired workers just for belonging to the union. But the labor movement developed a strong bond of solidarity; every union stood ready to help another union. The members of the Department Store Union were involved in other strikes, on other picket lines. I remember a group of us going down to the seamen's picket line and to the National Biscuit Company strike. We worked with the Transport Workers, the Fur Workers, the Drug and Hospital Union, and so many others. We helped each other on the union picket lines, and all of us always turned up at the political demonstrations. We had a deep sense of comradeship, of solidarity. I guess we knew that our unity made us strong.

2. The Threat of Fascism

WHILE AMERICANS WERE CONCENTRATING on domestic problems and Congress was debating measures to meet the crises, Europe was falling into chaos. On January 30, 1933, Adolf Hitler was made chancellor of Germany, and on March 23 the German Reichstag placed absolute power in his hands. Berlin became the ideological center of fascism, providing an example for Japan and inspiration for Italy, which had adopted fascism ten years earlier.

Hitler's National Socialist Party began its reign of terror by outlawing Germany's political parties, democratic institutions and movements, and the once-powerful and class-conscious trade unions. The Nazis would stop at nothing to achieve their ultimate goal of a world dominated by Aryans, with Jews, Blacks, Gypsies, and all other racial and political "undesirables"—communists, socialists, social democrats, and liberals—exterminated or enslaved. The burning of the Reichstag, Germany's house of parliament, an act engineered by the Nazis themselves, was blamed on the communists. This deliberate and premeditated act paved the way for the savage persecution of Jews and communists in particular. Through torture, murder, and the chilling threat of the concentration camps, the Nazis effectively tightened control and suppressed all opposition.

In 1934 I became interested in foreign affairs, especially what was going on in Germany. Hitler was in power, and the Nazi storm troopers were on the loose.

In those days, before television, we got our visual news from the newsreels in the movie houses. I remember to this day the vivid, cruel scenes of the Nazi storm troopers, with the swastika emblem on their sleeves, dragging Jewish people out of their shops, spitting on them, mocking them, trampling and kicking them with their shiny boots. I remember the book burnings. Those newsreel pictures made a deep impression on me. Hitler was so dangerous, I believed the whole world could be destroyed.

I joined many anti-fascist demonstrations. Once I was at the waterfront where Germany's largest passenger ship had docked. About ten thousand people were there shouting anti-Nazi slogans. At one point a young fellow got aboard the ship, climbed the main flagpole, tore down the huge Nazi swastika flag, and flung it into the water. The roar of the crowd swelled to a tremendous pitch. That young man was Bill Bailey, who later joined the Lincoln Battalion in Spain.

Another time, a fellow named Jack Corrigan—whom I also met later in Spain—climbed the Eternal Light flagpole at Twenty-third Street and Fifth Avenue in New York City. On top of the pole he hung a huge banner with an anti-Nazi slogan—"Free Ernst Thaelmann!"[1] On the way down he greased the flagpole, dipping into a can strapped to his back.

The next day, with thousands of spectators cheering the anti-Nazi banner waving in the breeze, one policeman after another tried to climb the pole. Of course, it was impossible. As each policeman tried and failed to climb the pole, the crowd cheered because the banner could wave a little longer. Finally, a fire engine came with ladders, and the banner was ripped off.

On February 16, 1936, the Popular Front government of the Spanish Republic was brought to power by a majority mandate. The new democratic government promised a brighter future for the Spanish people. But only a few months later, on July 18, Generals Franco, Sanjurjo, and Mola, together with the Spanish Falange, led the armed forces of Spain into rebellion against the young republic.

Fighting quickly spread to every province and major city of the Spanish mainland. Italy sent soldiers—almost one hundred thousand by war's end—and bombers to aid Franco's fascists. Germany also sent planes, as well as twenty thousand soldiers, including tank crews, pilots, and artillery and communications specialists using German-supplied armaments. Portugal sent two complete divisions of its regular army. Troops also were brought in from Africa—all to aid Franco. France, under British direction, invited the European nations to join in a common policy of nonintervention, and on August 8, 1936, France closed its frontier to Spain. Germany, Italy, and Portugal agreed "in principle" to nonintervention, but, needless to say, proceeded to arm and aid the Spanish insurgents as rapidly as possible.

During the summer of 1936, I was working at a small resort in the Catskills. One Sunday morning a guest came in for breakfast with the New York *Daily News.* The headline read: "Revolution in Spain!" I was a little confused, because I knew that a popular front government had recently been elected in Spain. After reading the article I realized it would have made more sense if the headline had read: "Counter-Revolution in Spain!" It was the military and the fascist Falange who were trying to overthrow the legally elected popular front government.

The situation held my interest from then on, and I followed the events in Spain daily. I knew that the fascists were in control in Germany and Italy, with close ties to the governments of Britain and Portugal, and with many powerful friends in the United States and France. Soon it became clear that Germany and Italy were behind the rebellion in Spain. If they won, what a boost to fascism all over the world, including the United States! I worried about it and read all the newspaper accounts avidly.

With the end of summer, my job at the resort was terminated, and there were no other jobs available, so I decided to ship out. I signed up as a steward on the *Express,* a freighter with a crew of about forty, and seven passengers. The trip took three months with stops at ports along the Mediterranean and the Black Sea.

During the entire trip, members of the crew discussed two events: the seamen's strike that had begun a week after we left New York, and the war in Spain. Feelings were very intense about both issues. We held numerous meetings and sent resolutions back home endorsing the strike and supporting the Loyalist cause in Spain. I met several of these seamen later in Spain.

The *Express* returned to the States in early January 1937. Almost immediately I learned that a few of my YCL and Local 1250 friends had gone to Spain to fight with the International Brigades against Franco. I wanted to go, and a friend of mine went with me to a place on Second Avenue, where a group of doctors examined us and other people questioned us to see if we really were anti-fascist. This committee was very somber and serious. They wanted us to know what we were getting into. One of them said something like, "You know, comrades, this is not just another picket line. This is a matter of life and death." I knew what he was saying and understood his message, but I could not forget those newsreels of the Nazi storm troopers stomping and spitting on those poor, helpless people. I also knew it *could* happen here. My anger was so strong, I knew I had to go. Fascism simply had to be stopped.

While the governments of Britain, France, and then the United States made concession after concession to fascism, volunteers came from all over the world to aid the Spanish people. They understood what their governments refused to acknowledge: that fascism must be stopped in Spain. The alternative was a second and more disastrous world war.

Some forty thousand men and women, including three thousand Americans, volunteered for the International Brigades. They were students, teachers, writers, trade unionists; most of them were communists, some were socialists. They all shared a hatred of fascism, a love of liberty.

So, on a cold February evening in 1937, I attended a special gathering in a New York City tenement. It was the night before I was scheduled to leave for Spain, and my group had been called together for last-minute instructions. About twenty-five volunteers attended. The atmosphere was eerie; the electric lights had faltered and then gone out. Candles were lit, casting shadows around the room and making the meeting seem somewhat conspiratorial.

The chairman opened the meeting, speaking slowly, obviously trying to impress us with the importance of his message.

"Your boat sails tomorrow at noon. Everyone is to be on board no later than eleven in the morning. You will be divided into groups of five. Each group will have a leader."

He paused and his gaze slowly drifted around the room.

"You understand that no one is to know where you are going. Make up excuses for your parents, relatives, and friends. No one is to know that you are going to Spain. Of course this means that you must come to the boat alone. Once on board, you must not draw attention to yourselves. Be inconspicuous. You are to mingle in groups of twos or threes. Be wary of your conversations, and do not discuss Spain or politics in general. There may be government agents aboard whose purpose is to prevent you from getting to Spain."

Now he became even more solemn.

"No one is to drink any hard liquor. The five dollars you will receive is for cigarettes and tips. This applies to your stay in France also. And please, no women! Anyone caught drunk, or found to have visited a prostitute in France, will be prohibited from entering Spain. He will be sent back to the States and will be considered a disgrace to the working class."

A few small necessities like shaving sets and toothbrushes were then distributed, and we left the room.

It was cold outside. I walked alone along Fourteenth Street until I came to Second Avenue. I slowed my pace as I headed downtown to Delancey Street.

So many times I had spoken as a member of the YCL on these street corners. I remembered my first experience as a street-corner speaker. The night before, I had spent hours in the privacy of my bathroom, staring at myself in the mirror, trying to memorize a three-minute speech. I couldn't sleep all night.

The next evening, at the rally, when I was introduced to the crowd of about thirty people, half of them members of my YCL club, I had butterflies in my stomach. I began my speech, talking in a very low voice. At first, the people came closer to hear me; then they began to drift away. Suddenly a policeman appeared. He was determined to break up the already dwindling crowd.

"End this meeting!" he roared. "You are breaking the law by using a torn American flag."

I looked down at him and shouted, "This tattered flag is more representative of the American people than a new flag! Look across the street where unemployed, homeless people are living in cardboard shacks with their children. Can't you see their clothes are torn, just like this flag? Why don't you worry about their torn clothes?"

A roar went up from the crowd, which suddenly seemed to be getting larger. They shouted, "Let him speak! He's right. That torn flag is our flag!"

The policeman left, and I continued with my speech to a now thoroughly appreciative audience.

My thoughts drifted to other memories. Here was Stanton Street, with those five-story, rat-infested tenements. It was on this street that I had helped carry furniture back into apartments after poverty-stricken families had been evicted.

There was the Magistrates Court on Second Avenue and Sixth Street. I had been on trial there so many times during department store strikes!

These streets had been my education, my life. I brushed away the thought that I might never be here again.

The next morning was cloudy and very cold. My mother was busily preparing breakfast. I had already told her that I had enlisted as a seaman and was embarking on a trip that would take at least three months, perhaps longer. I realized that if the war lasted more than three months, I would have to send her an additional travelog. Mom was cheerful that morning. She kept reminding me to be careful and to write to her from every port. She walked me to the door, kissed me, and peered into my eyes.

"Tell me the truth, Herschel. Are you going to Spain?"

Her perception and the abruptness of her question left me speechless for a second.

"What's the matter with you, Mom? Are you crazy? Me go to a war? Do I look like a lunatic? No, no, I am going on a long trip and will be back in three months. Now, don't worry about me."

After another quick kiss, I left in a hurry.

I walked rapidly through Tompkins Square Park and felt relieved that the departure from my mother had been relatively easy. My sister, Sal, lived with her family a few blocks away. I headed for her house for more farewells.

My brother-in-law, Hy, was getting ready to leave for work when I arrived.

"I'll walk you to the streetcar, Hy, and we can have a few last words," I told him. He was sad, and seemed on the verge of tears.

As we walked, Hy said, "You're coming back, Harry. They can't kill you."

"Of course I'll be back," I responded with forced enthusiasm.

"Harry, write to us at least once a week. Just a few words each time, letting us know you are alive and well."

"I'll write as often as I can. I may not be able to write as often as I'd like, and I'm sure letters will be censored. If I write that the weather is bad, you'll know that things are going badly for us, and if I write that the weather is sunny and good, then things are going well for us."[2]

Before Hy got on the streetcar, he gripped my hand, looked into my face for a few seconds, and said: "Please Harry, come back. We need you here."

My heart was heavy when I got back to Sal's. She and her twelve-year-old daughter, Louise, weren't any more cheerful than Hy.

Finally it was time to leave. Sal insisted on coming to the boat with me. I compromised: "ok, come to within a block of the boat, but no farther." Sal agreed, and we took a taxi to Tenth Avenue. I got out quickly, waved to Sal, and walked rapidly toward the huge ship in the harbor.

There it was—the *Ile de France,* the ship that would take me to Le Havre. I found my way to the third-class passenger entrance. To my surprise there were about three hundred men, all young, waiting in line. Ordinarily, at this time of the year, there would be but a few dozen third-class passengers. All of us in line were wearing old coats and carrying identical suitcases. Hardly inconspicuous!

As the line moved slowly toward the gangplank, I noticed several men walking quietly alongside us, speaking softly with the passengers. They were so well dressed that I immediately knew they were government agents. One of them approached me.

"Where are you going, young man?" he asked.

"I'm headed for the Alps. I want to do a bit of skiing."

"Are you sure it's the Alps and not the Pyrenees?"

"No, I like the Alps."

The man glared at me.

"It's strange how many of you guys are getting off welfare to go skiing in the Alps." He moved away and stopped the fellow in front of me. This comrade was hatless, his hair was uncombed, and his coat looked like it had seen quite a few winters.

"And where are you going?"

"To France."

"Why?"

"I'm going to write a book about France."

"A writer, eh? Gonna write a book about France. Very, very interesting. Isn't it Spain you're going to write about? Aren't you going to Spain?"

"Me? No sir, not me. There's a war going on there, bullets flying all over that country. I'm not going there! Not me! I'm writing a book about peaceful France."

"OK kid, write your book . . . but watch out for the bullets anyway."

At last I was on the ship. The deck was crowded with relatives and sweethearts of third-class passengers—comrade volunteers. So much for anonymity! Why hadn't I taken someone to the ship? I felt very lonely.

"I thought you weren't allowed to bring anyone," said a familiar voice behind my right shoulder. There was Sal, smiling at me, and beside her was my old friend Nat Lieber, who was the brother of Sal's husband, Hy. We sat down and talked, but before too long, all visitors were asked to leave.

At noon the ship started out of the port. I ran to the crowded railing and managed to get a look at the dock. There must have been a thousand people there, looking up and waving to us. Suddenly a few clenched fists shot up, then more and more, until I could no longer see any faces.

I returned to the cabin below, where I met my three bunkmates: Frank, a cab driver; Ralph, a gas station attendant; and John, a student from the University of Chicago. Another young man aboard ship, Robert Colodny, spent a lot of time in our cabin.

Our discussions were fascinating. Frank Chesler and I talked about the strikes we'd been involved in and the many fights we'd had with cops. Ralph, a twenty-one-year-old Italian-American, had spent most of his young life in pool halls. I was very impressed with the way he talked out of the side of his mouth. I had never seen anyone do that so nicely. Who would have dreamed that he would one day be the world-famous artist Ralph Fasanella!

John Murra was Romanian by birth and had been imprisoned in Romania as a teenager for left-wing activities. He had managed to escape and had made his way to the United States. We discovered that we had a mutual friend, Joan Michelson, who, like John, was also a student at the University of Chicago, and who was the daughter of Clarina Michelson, my union president.

Both John and Bob later carved distinguished careers in their respective fields: John Murra in anthropology, and Bob Colodny in history.

The voyage proved to be uneventful, although many rumors floated around the ship. The "Don't Trust Anyone Over Thirty" dictum didn't start in the 1960s; it seemed that anybody in third class with even the slightest tinge of gray in his hair had to be a spy or a government agent. There were about a dozen such people among us, and we whispered warnings to each other about them. It was a pleasant surprise to meet these "spies" later in the trenches in Spain.

Seven days after we left New York, the ship docked at Le Havre. I suppressed my excitement, trying to appear nonchalant and to act like a seasoned traveler.

Soon all the third-class passengers were crowded into a room where we awaited our visas. Finally, the steward came, accompanied by a Frenchman and an American diplomat. They looked us over, placed themselves around a table, and called the first name on their list.

"How much money do you have?" asked the American diplomat.

"About five dollars," answered a very surprised young man.

"Five dollars! How can you travel with so little money?"

"I plan to wire home for money."

"I see. Well, we will hold your passport until then. Meanwhile, wait in that room."

A few more men were questioned along similar lines. They also were sent to another room without their passports. We realized that we were being questioned alphabetically, so those whose names were at the beginning of the alphabet dashed around to the others to borrow as much money as they could for just several minutes. The next few men had from thirty to forty dollars. The diplomat seemed surprised. Not to be outdone, he now began to mark the money as it was shown to him. After that, the men called up again had only five dollars, or no money at all. They also were sent to the adjoining room without their passports. Now the diplomat was tired of it all. He stood up and called for order.

"Let's be honest with each other," he cooed. "We know just where all of you are going. Perhaps you are going with the best of intentions, but you are wasting your time. We know you are trying to go to Spain, but it is too late now. The border has been closed by the French government. And in case you didn't notice, let me tell you that all of your passports are stamped 'Not Valid for Travel in Spain.' Now, this ship is returning to New York in three days. Anyone who wants to return is to report to the American consulate, and he will be put on this ship without any cost to him. That is all. We will now return your passports."

No one accepted his offer.

In half an hour I was off the ship; a few hours later our group arrived by bus in Paris. Dave "Mooch" Engels, Harry Hakim, Maynard Goldstein, and I taxied to the hotel to which we had been assigned. Harry Hakim went out to see what French women were like, and the rest of us went to sleep.

The next day, following instructions, we attended a meeting at a clubhouse located in a working-class section of Paris. Each day we congregated at the same clubhouse, carried on discussions, and nervously anticipated the day we would leave for Spain. For a while it looked as though we would never leave Paris—the socialist government of France had indeed closed the border. So here we were, about three hundred Americans, milling around, waiting anxiously and impatiently for the order to leave.

Meanwhile, another boatload of volunteers arrived from the United States. One day, seven of these new men joined our group. They called themselves the "Debs Column." They had been sent over by the American Socialist Party. Their leader was a tall, thin, middle-aged man, with a kind, rough, Abe Lincoln–type face. His name was Hans Amlie. He had been an officer in the U.S. Army and had been stationed in France during World War I. Another Debs Column volunteer was Sam Romer, who had attended Commonwealth College with me some years earlier.

Pat Reid was another of the seven in the Debs Column. He too was an experienced soldier, having served three years with the British army during the First World War. Pat had also fought with the IRA against the British during the Irish Revolution. Some time after that he had emigrated to the United States to avoid arrest by the British and had become an American citizen. Pat was about five foot five; Hans was about six foot three. The two were always together, and always arguing, although it was evident that they had a great deal of respect for each other. Hans was a socialist, and Pat was an anarchist, perhaps the only American anarchist who fought in Spain.

On our eighth morning in Paris, twenty people were told to pack and get ready to leave. John Murra was one of the twenty. The rest of us gathered around them, trying to find out what their orders were, but they wouldn't answer. From the excitement on their faces, we assumed they were headed for Spain.

The next day thirty more names were called; mine was one of them. We had a few hours to get packed and be at headquarters, ready to move. Others in my group included Mooch Engels, Pat Reid, Hans Amlie, Maynard Goldstein, Harry Hakim, and John Oscar Bloom, a Canadian whom we came to know as "Red."

At headquarters, the thirty men were divided into groups of five. Each group left separately for the railroad station. It was very crowded when we got there. The French passengers, though curious about the groups of young men milling around, said nothing, but looked at us with slight smiles and warm eyes. We, on the other hand, were very nervous that our identities would be revealed and that we might be arrested. It was with a tremendous sense of relief that we finally boarded the train, even though it was old and uncomfortable.

All night, as the train headed south, we gathered in small groups, and in hushed tones talked about Spain and the future.

The next day dawned sunny and warm. I opened my window and

gazed out at the flat and colorless land, but the smell of spring was in the air; it was beautiful. I saw my first French grapevines, and later, miles of them.

Our instructions were very clear. My group was to get off the train near Perpignan, take a bus to town, and wait at a certain restaurant for further instructions. When the train pulled in, we learned that the bus was due in about an hour. A few of us went into a restaurant near the train station for coffee. Before long a few townspeople came in, looked us over, and approached us with questions.

"They want to know if we're going to Spain," said one of our boys who understood French.

"No," he answered for us, "we are just touring the southern part of France. We are students from an American university."

The townspeople smiled and nodded knowingly.

"Many students from many countries are passing through here every day," one of them said in broken English.

"Good luck," said another. "This is our fight too."

Later, on the bus, the other passengers smiled at us, waved clenched fists, or patted us on the back as they got off.

We arrived in Perpignan later that morning. Everything looked so peaceful! I spent several hours walking around the town and noticed the many posters plastered on the walls; most of them were pro-Loyalist, but some were pro-fascist. Under a ¡Viva Franco! slogan there would be two posters with ¡Viva España Republicana! At six o'clock that evening, ten of us, representing two groups, met in the designated restaurant.

Mooch told us to keep ordering food, because we had to wait there for our contact to appear. We ate and ate and ate some more.

Finally, in walked our contact, John Murra. John, who spoke many languages fluently, had been asked to work with the committee that was responsible for getting the Internationals into Spain. (Josip Broz Tito was in charge of this committee; after the war he became president of Yugoslavia.)

John explained that we were going to be part of the first American group to attempt to climb the Pyrenees into Spain. He warned us that this was not going to be easy. The border between France and Spain had just been closed by the French government, and the number of border guards had been greatly increased. We were to leave the restaurant, and in exactly thirty minutes were to be about a mile away, where we would be met by two taxicabs. Mooch had the license plate numbers in his hand.

We were to leave the restaurant one at a time, keeping about thirty feet apart, and always watching the man walking directly ahead. And, as always, we were to be as inconspicuous as possible. So there we were, a steady single file of ten young men, each carrying the same cardboard suitcase, with eyes riveted ahead, trying to look casual! Our pace was set by Mooch, the leader of the group; when he walked slowly, we all slowed down; when he picked up speed, so did we. Once, Mooch stopped in front of a store display window to light a cigarette; unfortunately the rest of us had no window to look at. So we just stopped dead in our tracks and waited for Mooch to start walking again.

Suddenly, he looked at his watch and must have realized that we had been strolling too casually; he began to run. Naturally, we all ran right behind him—keeping our thirty-foot distance, of course. Hundreds of people, out for their evening walk, saw us. Some raised their clenched fists in salute and shouted "¡Viva España!" In the center of a cross street, a French policeman stopped traffic so that we could pass. He too raised his hand in a clenched-fist salute. Everyone seemed to know who we were and where we were going.

Finally, out of breath, we arrived at our destination and found the cabs waiting for us. We quickly piled in. Within seconds the cabs took off. We drove for a few miles before getting off the paved road. Now we were on what looked like a cart path. The drivers dimmed their lights and continued to drive up a hill. Every so often I saw the lead driver flick his headlights on and off, obviously signaling to someone. An answering light flickered in the distance. About a half hour later the cabs stopped.

A small group of men were sitting on the ground in a circle, evidently waiting for us. Altogether there were thirty of us who would climb the Pyrenees in the darkness of night. A Frenchman, a smuggler by trade, with a dog by his side, was our guide. The dog, we were told, would stay at the end of the line and would remain with anyone who was unable to complete the journey until help arrived. We were asked not to smoke and not to speak in loud voices.

The walk started easily enough; the night air was warm and pleasant. After about an hour the hills became steeper and more treacherous. It was beginning to get colder, and it was difficult to keep warm. After a few more hours, the hills became even steeper, and the ground turned white from a recent snowstorm. Everyone was huffing and puffing and needing help to maneuver on some of the slippery spots. Pat Reid, older than the rest of us, was undaunted, spirited, and energetic. He kept encouraging us over the rough spots.

After six hours of this, I was exhausted. The snow was not deep, but in many places the ground was icy and slippery. I wanted to stop to rest and sleep. But I saw the others struggling, slipping, getting bruised and scratched, yet still going on. I couldn't stop. So I pushed ahead, climbing, slipping, falling, and freezing.

Finally, just before dawn, the guide stopped us, put his fingers to his lips, and sat us down around him. Quietly, he explained that we were less than half a mile from the Spanish border, but that there were many unfriendly French guards around us. We would have to proceed with extreme caution.

The walking was much easier now, as we were going slightly downhill. We all seemed to have miraculously regained our energy and enthusiasm.

And then a white house appeared just ahead. Our guide began running. One by one we broke into a run just behind him.

Spain! We were on Spanish soil!

We raised our clenched fists and shouted "¡Viva España!" We began to sing "The Internationale," quietly, a little self-consciously at first, then louder and louder. It was a moment I will never forget.

We were the first American group to climb the Pyrenees into Spain, but we would not be the last.

3. Spain

Arise ye prisoners of starvation!
Arise ye wretched of the earth!
For justice thunders condemnation,
A better world's in birth.
——"The Internationale"

WE HAD COMPLETED OUR TREK through the Pyrenees and had arrived at the ancient Catalan town of Figueras. It was February 1937. There were thirty of us from the United States who, along with about two hundred other Internationals, were housed in a fortress with a tremendous moat and drawbridge. Before the war's end its walls would be inscribed with the names and hometowns of hundreds of Americans, along with their thoughts while awaiting battle. Here we would receive our basic training.

On our second day in Figueras we were divided into groups of twenty to begin drill exercises. Because of his World War I experience, Pat Reid was named drill master of our group. But Pat was an anarchist and didn't believe in drilling. As a result, our group would often sit around in a circle, listening to Pat relate his experiences. None of us believed a word he said, but I liked Pat's stories and took to him immediately. Pat liked me as well, probably because I appreciated his ramblings. Fortunately, despite Pat's anarchism, we did complete about ten days of intensive drilling and marching, and practiced attacks on nearby hills.

Each morning we went on maneuvers, and each night we gathered in a damp, underground room. Here I met other International volunteers —anti-fascist Germans, Italians, Hungarians, French, and many others. The unfamiliar languages made conversation rather difficult, but music—especially revolutionary songs—brought forth warm smiles and vigorous handshakes.

The morning maneuvers were consistent—we had to "capture" a hill, the same hill, day after day. We would start by forming a single line about a half mile in front of the hill; we had to fall often and hard, as bullets were supposedly flying all around us. The ground leading to the hill was rocky and thorny, so we got cut and scratched and bruised each time we fell. At the foot of the hill, panting like crazy, we would wait for the whistle that would send us dashing up the steep slope, screaming at the top of our lungs. I suppose the noise was meant to scare the enemy, but I couldn't help wondering what would happen if the enemy screamed louder than we did. So I never yelled. The shouting would always stop about halfway up, and from then on all you could hear was grunting. At the top, we just sat, puffing away, and hoping that if we ever confronted the enemy in a similar situation, they would forget how to shoot, because we'd be too exhausted to fight. When we returned to the bottom of the hill, the French officer in charge of the fort would lecture us and point out all of our mistakes—and every day they were the same. We didn't fall fast enough; we worried too much about scratches and not enough about getting killed; our dash up the hill was more like playing a game than fighting a war.

Each day, after our typical lunch of beans, beans, and more beans, we would take a siesta and then march to the town of Figueras, where we would be dismissed for two hours to do as we pleased—except patronize prostitutes, which nevertheless became a favorite pastime.

What I remember most about our daily marches from the fort to Figueras was the interaction between Pat Reid and a German-American comrade named Herman Bottcher. Being an anarchist, Pat refused to take orders or give them and was opposed to discipline of any kind. Herman believed that an army had to have leaders, structure, and rules. As we'd march to town, Pat would always, intentionally, be out of step. Herman bawled the hell out of him, but his reprimands were in vain.

"You can't win a war without a disciplined army," Herman shouted.

"Your German army was pretty disciplined in the world war," Pat retorted. "How come it lost?"

Herman softened a bit and agreed. "That's a good point. The trouble was that the Germans didn't know what they were fighting for. You must believe in what you're fighting for and also have discipline. Then you can't lose."

For the most part I agreed with Herman, but I still admired Pat and his always egalitarian point of view.[1]

It was sometimes difficult to remember that Figueras was part of Spain; it didn't seem to be a town at war. Even the white tape on the windows, used to prevent shattering in the event of a bombing, was patterned into beautiful designs. The people of Figueras behaved as if they were a community in peacetime. Because this area was home to many anarchists who believed that *any* Spanish government didn't represent them, young men were plentiful. The town sympathized with the popular front and hoped we would defeat the fascists, but they were determined to stay out of the fight unless the fascists entered their part of the country, Catalonia. There were exceptions among the Catalans, most notably Buenaventura Durruti. Durruti was a popular leader who organized a large group of anarchists into a military unit. He was killed at the Madrid front while courageously leading his group against the fascists.

One night, the Americans were called into the damp, underground room for a special meeting. Comrade Allan Johnson, a dignified man who had once been a captain in the U.S. Army, spoke to us.[2]

"Comrades," Johnson began, "we are leaving tomorrow morning for the International Brigade headquarters in Albacete. We are not going to the front just yet, but we are going to receive intensive training." We all cheered with real enthusiasm. At last we were getting near the real thing. My heart raced; we were too naive to be scared.

"And I have some news from the front concerning the Americans," Johnson continued. A hush fell over the room. We knew there were several hundred Americans who had arrived in Spain before us, and until this moment we hadn't heard a word about them.

"The American battalion has lived up to, and surpassed, all expectations," Johnson said. "Our boys were victorious in a very important battle near Madrid [Jarama], a defensive battle, in which they stopped the fascists dead in their tracks." We all applauded, but only briefly, for we wanted to know more.

"I know you are waiting to hear about the casualties." He paused. "Only one American was killed and only four were wounded."

The cheering was loud and long. Only five casualties among about three hundred soldiers—and a big victory.

"¡Viva los americanos!" someone shouted, and we all hurrahed.

Johnson continued, "The Americans have named themselves 'the Lincoln Battalion.'"

"Three cheers for the Lincoln Battalion!" We cheered ourselves hoarse.

"Three cheers for the International Brigades!" More cheers.

"Three cheers for España Republicana!" Still more cheers.

We went to bed exhausted after all the celebrating. The next day we were going to central Spain, where all the action was.

The train ride to Albacete was slow and long, but our brief stops along the way proved to be inspiring. In every town we were met at the station by a delegation from the Popular Front. The stations were crowded with cheering workers, peasants, and schoolchildren. We would flock to the open windows, wave our clenched fists, return their cheers, and catch the oranges they threw to us. Oranges were plentiful at that time of year.

But it was disheartening to see the hunger on the faces of the people. Children would come to the train with their hands out, crying, "pan, pan." We threw bread to them, and the children rushed back to their mothers to display their prizes.

After we had passed a few stations, we each had a basketful of oranges, and by the next morning, the train was so full of oranges, we were literally tripping over them in the aisles. The oranges were sweet and juicy. I must have eaten a few dozen that day, and the result was not very pleasant. Most of the boys, including me, got their first case of Spanish diarrhea. It was weeks before I would eat another orange.

When we arrived at Albacete, we were greeted by hundreds of school-children, shouting and singing. It was here that I saw my first signs of the war; bullet holes had pierced the cement buildings, and tremendous bomb craters dotted the streets. When the fascist revolt had erupted in July 1936, the Guardia Civil had taken control of this town for the fascists, and the civilians had fought for days before finally overpowering them.

At what had once been the Guardia Nacional barracks, we were marched into a tremendous mess room, where we received a simple but good meal. After eating, Johnson told us he was leaving for the Jarama front to join the Americans who had arrived earlier; he would report back to us in a few days. He then introduced the American base commissar, George Brodsky, who advised us to surrender our passports. They would remain in Albacete for safekeeping.

We then went into the drill yard where we were to pick up our army gear. Everything was neatly stacked in piles: shoes, brown army pants, jackets, shirts, socks, and ammunition pouches. We walked from pile to pile, picking out the things we needed. Before putting on our uniforms, we were able to take a shower, one of the very few times we had the opportunity in Spain.

The small towns surrounding Albacete were used by the International Brigades for training purposes. The Americans went to Madrigueras, where we were barracked in an unused warehouse. We spent the first few days just cleaning the place and making it a little more livable.

About one hundred Americans were at the base. The forty Americans who had been there earlier had already left for the Córdoba front, led by John Gates.

We were formed into a company of three sections. Hans Amlie was commander, Mooch Engels was elected company commissar, and Bill Hallowell was my section commander.

Hallowell was a forty-year-old Canadian professional soldier and World War I veteran. He explained that although he was a professional soldier, he fought only on the side he believed was right; this Spanish war was the most clear-cut war he had ever fought in.

Our section of thirty men spent about five or six hours every day being drilled by Hallowell. But we didn't learn very quickly, and Hallowell would not hesitate to curse us whenever someone was out of step (all too frequently). One day, after we had made a number of mistakes, he gathered us under a tree, and lectured us in a sarcastic, disgusted voice: "The whole bunch of you are nothing but a bunch of bloody cunts."

That evening, a group of us went to see Mooch, our commissar, and protested the treatment we were receiving from Hallowell.

"What the hell are you beefing about?" Mooch yelled. "This is an army, and you'd better get used to this language. Hallowell means well. He's been a soldier all his life and this is the only language he knows. Do you expect him to call you a bunch of bloody comrades? Get used to it. The fascists will do much more than throw cuss words at you."

We let it go at that. After a while, we did get used to it, and, somewhat grudgingly, we even began to like Hallowell. One thing was for sure: This wasn't a run-of-the-mill regular army—we finally began to cuss him right back. He'd just smile and you could almost hear him say, "Yeah, these kids are learning." He wasn't a bad guy.

After a few weeks, the number of Americans in Madrigueras had grown to about two hundred, and we were formed into two companies.

One day we were called to a special meeting in the theater. Robert Merriman, who had been commander of the Lincoln Battalion until he was wounded at the front, came to the training base with his arm still in a sling. Tall and dignified, Merriman had been an instructor of economics at the University of California at Berkeley; now he was accompanied by his wife, Marion,[3] and by Sam Stember, the commissar of the Lincolns.

Merriman and Stember gave us news of the front line. The Americans had participated in two important actions, one on February 23, and the other on February 27. The goal of these two actions had been to stop the fascist advance on Madrid, a struggle that had been going on for weeks. In neither attack did the Americans gain any ground, but they did manage to divert the fascists to such an extent that they stopped attacking. The actions, according to Merriman, received high praise from the Spanish general staff.

Stember talked about life in the trenches. The end of February and all of March had been rainy and cold. The men had slept in the mud, and there had been very little food. Stember criticized the few men who had grumbled and praised the great majority who had accepted all this in the right spirit. Naively, we expressed surprise that there was such a thing as "grumbling" in the battalion.

I admired Stember and Merriman, one just out of the hospital, the other fresh from the front. But some of the men listening to Stember resented the way he spoke about the "grumblers." What the hell, they said, fellows who have been through a battle have a right to do a little grumbling without being criticized. I tried to defend Stember, arguing that the men had to expect hardships, that grumbling was only a sign of weakness and maybe even insincerity.

"Wait until you've been to the front," I was told. "You'll do your share of grumbling."

How right they were!

Also about this time a handsome, well-built black man, Walter Garland, arrived at the training base. The Lincoln Battalion was the first American military outfit to be integrated. To us, there was nothing unusual about this—as leftists, most of our political and social clubs back home had been integrated. But the U.S. Army was to remain segregated throughout World War II, and until 1947.

Garland had been wounded on February 27 and still had a bullet in his midsection. He had been sent to teach us how to handle the Soviet-made rifles that were being used at the front. Unfortunately, there were only five rifles on the base, but we did the best we could.

The first day Garland was at the base, he was asked to speak to us. Everyone came to the meeting, anxious to hear stories of the front. I was thrilled by what he told us, of individual acts of bravery, of the suffering endured by the men, of the rough conditions with the rain and the cold, and in spite of it all, of the fine spirit of the men. He had us all enthralled, but frankly I suspected his heroic descriptions were lacking in reality.

After we had been at Madrigueras for three weeks, our training was intensified. For about a month we drilled and drilled; once, and only once, we went to the rifle range. I was given a rifle and was cautioned to hold the butt tight against my shoulder. It seemed very heavy. I lay flat on my stomach and pressed the rifle so tightly that my shoulder ached for days afterward.

A white handkerchief held aloft from the trench signaled the moment to fire. I fired and missed. The report was much louder than I had expected, and my heart beat a bit faster. I fired and missed again. Five times I fired, and five times I missed. Jeez, what the hell kind of a soldier would I be?! I should have hit the target at least once! But no. My record was perfect.

I wrote home often—as often as possible, mostly to my sister, Sal, her husband, Hy, and their young daughter, Louise. On April 10, 1937, I wrote:

Dear Sal and Hy:

We just received a batch of *Daily Workers* here up to March 25 and you should have seen the grab for them. The comrades are all sitting on their bunks reading and many are waiting for them to finish. I'm looking forward tonight to reading all the papers.

I read one article of March 24, I think, of the 5 & 10 strike. Gosh, you have no idea how glad it made me feel. If ever any place needed organization, 5 & 10 is the place. I suppose Sal, you've been pretty close to the strike. You've got to write me a detailed letter on how it turned out. Give Clarina my love.

I wish I could impress you with the friendship of the civilians here for the comrades of the Lincoln Battalion. Comrades are invited out every night for supper in the small, clay houses. They seem to feel it an honor to have us eat with them. You will never leave their house hungry, even if it means they have too little. One comrade told me of a woman, who noticing that he wore glasses and thinking that perhaps he couldn't shoot well, offered him a large knife to use against the fascists. Such hatred [for the fascists] you have never seen.

One thing you don't see is a hungry soldier. . . .

I remember this well—the Spanish people would not allow us to be hungry. Every day, when we returned from drill practice, a group of children would be waiting for us. We always had some candy for them. One little boy, about ten years old, was constantly by my side. He would smile broadly, and his eyes would brighten as I'd give him candy. One day he tried to tell me something; he made motions as though he were putting food into his mouth. I asked Julius Deutsch, a Texan who had lived in Mexico for some years and who spoke Spanish fluently, to translate for me. The youngster was trying to explain that his parents wanted me to come to their home for supper. I asked him if Julie could come along, and he assured me it was OK.

The child's house was at the other end of town. A low-built mud hut, it was located on a narrow street that could only accommodate carts. A few old chairs and one table were the only furniture in the house. There were no closets or dressers, beds, plumbing, sinks, toilets, electricity, or stove. The cooking was done in the fireplace. And there it was, our supper, a huge pot of beans and a large pan of fried eggs.

The boy's mother, looking worn and gaunt, greeted us warmly and cheerfully. She took my hand and thanked me for the candy I had given her son. There was another young child in the house, a girl of about seven, who was very shy and giggled every time I tried to speak to her. There was another daughter, María, who was about eighteen. She blushed when Julie and I came in, and said "salud" very shyly. She listened to our conversation but never said a word.

At about sundown, the father came in from the fields with his fifteen-year-old son, pulling their burro into the house. They led the burro through the dining room and into another room, which, I discovered later, was its very own. The odor of the burro lingered and mingled with the cooking odors.

After a little while the bean pot and the pan of eggs were placed on the table. On the side was a salad of cucumbers, scallions, and lettuce. Under the table was a large pan that contained the hot ashes from the fireplace to keep our feet warm.

We sat down and the mother, aware of American customs, gave Julie and me separate plates, while the family ate out of the frying pan and bean pot.

The father asked in broken English if we were Americans.

"Yes," we assured him.

"From North America?" he questioned.

"Yes, from los Estados Unidos."

"Things are very good in America, aren't they?"

"Well, things are very good for the rich, but not so good for the poor. There are about 15 million people who are unemployed, and many are hungry and homeless in the United States."

The father looked surprised. He couldn't believe that people could be poor in the United States.

"You have a good president," the father said, thinking that he was pleasing us. "Roosevelt is a good man."

Julie thought for a moment and then said, "Sometimes he's good and sometimes he's not so good."

"But he must be good," insisted the father. "Didn't he send you Americans here to help us win the fight against the fascists?"

Julie and I were both startled. We had heard that many Spaniards thought we had been sent by the United States government, but this was the first time it was expressed directly to us.

"We are volunteers, mostly communists, and we were not sent by our government. In fact, our government has done everything in its power to stop us from coming to help you. Even the French socialist government closed its borders to stop us from coming to Spain. We had to climb the Pyrenees to get here."

The mother beamed. We later learned that she was a communist and the father a socialist. The four children just listened, without saying a word.

Then they told us how grateful they were to the Spanish government for giving them the land that they had previously worked on. The land, formerly owned by the Catholic Church, was a few kilometers outside the town of Madrigueras. Every morning at sunrise, father and son left the house with the burro, to return only at sunset. The work was hard, they said, but now that they owned the land, it was rewarding.

After dinner, Julie and I accompanied the entire family to the center of town, where everyone strolled around the square in a huge circle. Other Americans were promenading, some of them holding hands with young girls—with the girls' parents walking close behind. I took María's hand and we continued to stroll, silently, but with occasional side glances. Julie walked with the rest of the family behind us, talking nonstop.

After that night, Julie and I frequently returned from drill practice to find the young son waiting to bring us home for dinner. It was fine to eat with a simple, honest family after being with the fellows all day. It made me feel that I belonged someplace. Occasionally, I would go by myself, English-Spanish dictionary in hand, and all through our conversations there would be long pauses while I looked up some word. Half of my talking was done with my hands, but somehow we did understand each other in spite of my poor Spanish.

One evening, the father took me aside. He asked me if I would marry María when the war was over. At first I thought he was joking, but he wasn't. I was very embarrassed; my face must have turned beet red, judging from the way he laughed. The father assured me that it was perfectly all right if I didn't like his daughter. But his neighbor had a very nice daughter, he continued: Would I like to meet her? I protested, saying that I did like María, but that right now I wasn't thinking of marriage. All this time, María sat quietly in a corner, her face very composed. I couldn't tell whether all this was embarrassing her. I felt so bad for her that I asked her if she would like to go to a movie Sunday night. She nodded yes.

That Sunday night when I came to call for her, I found the whole family dressed in their finest clothes. Sure enough the entire family accompanied us. María sat at one end of a row of seats, I at the other, and the family sat between us. Just an old Spanish custom, apparently.

One day in April a special meeting was called to give us the latest news from the front. We had heard that Italian fascist troops were fighting in Guadalajara and that our Spanish troops had routed them. We were anxious to hear the details. Captain Allan Johnson was at the meeting, and when he was introduced we all stood up and applauded. He spoke in a quiet, calm voice.

"The Americans were in a battle a few weeks ago [March 14], a quick battle that we won. The fascists had launched a surprise attack and captured part of the trench to our left. We sent a group to rout them and at the same time the main part of the battalion went over the top to attack their trenches. Although our men didn't take their trenches, we succeeded in routing them out of ours. Our comrades were in no-man's-land all day, but fortunately nearly all of them came back safely. We did lose five comrades, and seventeen were wounded, some slightly and some more seriously."

Johnson told us about Bob Raven, who had been seriously wounded. Raven was one of the group sent out to recapture the trench taken by the fascists. A grenade exploded at his feet; he lost both his eyes, and his body was badly cut. But, according to Johnson, his spirit was so good that he was propagandizing the nurses while he was being prepared for surgery. At least that was what we were told.

One of the commissars at the meeting then told Johnson that some of the fellows were complaining about the living conditions at the training base. Johnson wrinkled his forehead and said, "I'm surprised that anyone would complain about the conditions here. If you complain here, what will you do when you get to the front? Why, here you have mattresses and a roof over your head to protect you from the rain, while at the front the men are sleeping in the trenches in the mud and the freezing cold."

All of us were silent with shame.

He continued. "And let me tell you that many of you are going to be sent to the front in a very few days."

My heart thumped wildly. In just a few days I could be at the front!

Two days later a rumor started circulating that we would be leaving the next morning. Sure enough, that night all the lower officers were called to a special meeting. When they returned, we were told to pack up and be ready to move in the morning, or perhaps even during the night. Only forty of us were going; we were replacements for some of the casualties.

That night we sat around talking about what we could expect. We all got pretty sentimental, especially because many of the boys had a little too much to drink. Hallowell was drunk and furious when he learned he wasn't going to the front just yet; he was needed at the base to train the new men who were soon to arrive.

I didn't sleep very well that night. When everything was quiet and dark, my excitement turned to nervousness and worry. My mind kept returning to one particular scene from *All Quiet on the Western Front,* in which a German soldier, played by Lou Ayres, stabbed a French soldier, then stared at him as he lay dying. Next to the dying French soldier was a photo of his family. Even in death the French soldier's eyes were riveted on the German.

I finally fell asleep and dreamed that I was on a battlefield with hundreds of my comrades, all dead, and the fascists were combing the field, looking for live bodies to stab with their bayonets. I remained motionless, pretending to be dead. A fascist came and stood over me, lifted his bayonet . . . and I awoke in a cold sweat.

I was miserable, scared, and shaking and wished I were back home. I couldn't sleep the rest of the night. Many of the others were moving and moaning in their sleep, and I knew that they were having similar nightmares.

The next morning, an hour before dawn, my group lined up in the main square. Each of us was given a day's rations, a large can of bully beef, hard biscuits, and a small loaf of bread.

Even though we had been told not to let anyone know we were leaving for the front, I had told María and her family the night before, only to discover that they already knew. The whole town knew, and practically everyone came to see us off. I tried to give María's mother fifty pesetas; after all, they had been feeding me and doing my laundry for three weeks. But they refused to take anything, and instead gave me a bag containing hard-boiled eggs, bread, a jar of cooked fruit, and some sausage. Other Americans also were getting bags of food from other Spanish families. The Spaniards were sad; many were crying, especially the older people. They acted as though we were their children going off to the front. When the trucks began to move, we all sang "The Internationale," and they joined in with their clenched fists raised high above their heads.

4. *Jarama*

ABOUT AN HOUR LATER we arrived at the Fifteenth Brigade headquarters at Morata de Tajuna. The day was warm and clear; everything was strangely peaceful. I noticed the buds beginning to blossom and listened to the birds chirping in the treetops. The war seemed remote.

Lieutenant-Colonel Klaus, an anti-fascist German officer who was second in command of the Fifteenth Brigade, welcomed us. He tersely explained that the front had been quiet for the past few weeks, but warned that fighting could begin at any time. He cautioned us to be constantly on guard. After Klaus finished his brief talk, another officer tried to determine if any among us had any special talents. Was anyone multilingual? Did anyone have any experience in the use of machine guns? Were there any transmissions men, telephone men?

Pat Reid spoke up. Yes, he said, he had experience in transmissions.

"Where and when?"

"Three years with the British army in the world war."

"OK, if we need you, we will let you know."

Just then two trucks arrived to take us from Brigade headquarters to the kitchen of the Lincoln Battalion, where the smell of potatoes and olive oil filled the air. Jack Shirai was the cook for the Lincolns at that time. A Japanese-American from California, he had been a chef back home, and a damn good one. He did things with garbanzos that made them taste better than any garbanzos I ever had.

Jack had two good friends in Spain, Mel Offsink and Max Krauthamer. I sat in on many of their bull sessions. My favorites were those in which they'd talk about their plans for the future. After the war, they were going to open a restaurant together, and anyone who had fought in Spain would never have to pay for a meal. They would soak the rich and open their kitchen to the poor. Shirai took pleasure in describing the food they would serve, the delicacies he would make. We listened in sweet agony.

After finishing a satisfying meal, we were each given 150 rounds of ammunition; our pouches sagged and felt very heavy. We got in line and began marching, single file, along the side of the road, heading for the Jarama front. We were cautioned to keep a good distance between ourselves, just in case the enemy began shelling.

My heart was thumping wildly as I realized I was getting close to the front. And an hour later we were there. Moments after I arrived, I met a comrade from back home, Irving Chocheles, a fellow union member. At last! I was so glad to see someone I knew, someone who had already had battle experience!

Irv gave me a detailed account of the February 23 and 27 attacks. The fighting had been fierce and bloody; Irv was still deeply shaken. Only ninety of the four hundred men who had come to Jarama the week before had survived the battle.

"Harry, it's been hell. I've seen men die; I've seen them cut to pieces; I've seen men badly wounded, with their guts hanging out, some with their heads practically blown off."

"Wait a minute, Irv. We were told that there were very few casualties, that you guys had achieved tremendous victories."

"Bull. We had the shit knocked out of us."

He paused.

"We came to Jarama full of enthusiasm. On the second day we were told the time had come to chase those fascists away from Madrid, and we were ready to do just that.

"We were told to go over the top screaming and yelling, and that that would surely scare the hell out of the fascists. We were so inexperienced we believed it! We put our knapsacks on our backs, put the bayonets in our rifles, and when the order came to attack, we were like a bunch of boy scouts, the good guys chasing the bad guys. In seconds, we were chopped down. Many were killed immediately and dozens were wounded. We had expected artillery support, but there was nothing.

"We went over the top screaming and yelling at the top of our lungs," he continued. "It didn't scare the fascists. Oh, the screaming continued for a long time, but it was from the wounded stuck out in no-man's-land. And then, Harry, we went through the same thing again four days later. And again we had no artillery support and again the casualties were heavy.

"The men are angry. We all feel that we should have had better training. Some of us didn't even have rifles but charged anyway, thinking that the screams and shouts would frighten away the fascists. It was just plain slaughter."

We had talked for about an hour when Irv introduced me to some of the veterans of the Jarama battles. First was Hy Stone, a quiet, serious, very young-looking fellow who didn't seem to be as upset as Chocheles. I told Hy that I had met his two brothers, Joe and Sam, still in training, in Madrigueras. We talked for a while about his brothers. I liked Hy. We had something in common—we had both been raised in orphanages. Then there was Charlie Nusser, a tall, thin, cheerful guy, always ready with a quip and a laugh. He also was not as upset as Irv.

"Do you remember Sid Crotto, who worked with us during the Ohrbach's strike?" Irv asked.

"Sure, where is he?"

"He's in the trenches right now, on a machine-gun squad. Come with me."

I knew that I'd have to get into a trench sooner or later, so I mustered up all my courage and followed him. We walked through a communication trench, and in less than a minute we came upon a machine-gun crew. There was Sid, greeting me with a big grin and a warm handshake, just as if we were back on Fourteenth Street in New York City.

"Want to take a look at the fascist trenches?" Sid asked.

"Oh, I don't need to see those bastards," I said, unable to hide my nervousness.

"Nothing to be scared of," Sid laughed. "Come on, here's the peephole."

The peephole looked large enough for a shell to come through, and I didn't like the idea of looking through it. But I took a quick look and saw what appeared to be a line of sandbags about one hundred yards away.

"Yes sir, over there, just a stone's throw away are the guys that are waiting to kill us," Sid said softly. "Would you like to see me hit their trenches, just to let them know that we are still here? Take a look."

And sure enough he opened up with his machine gun, and I saw the dust rise from the fascist sandbags.

Later that evening, a group of us gathered in a circle. The "old-timers," those who had been in action, told the rest of us about the events that had taken place on February 27.

One day before, the men had been told that they were going to attack in the morning. At midnight, a group of eighty newly arrived Americans joined them. None of the new men had ever shot—or even held—a rifle. They were given rifles and bullets and were told to be ready to attack in a few hours. The new fellows were spirited and enthusiastic, ready to do anything they were ordered to do.

The battalion had been told that before the attack our artillery would knock the hell out of the fascist trenches, our airplanes would bomb them, and our tanks would move in front of the foot soldiers.

It sounded very good, but nothing like that occurred. Two of our planes had appeared at dawn, looked around, and then returned to their base. There was no artillery, and two tanks stayed behind the lines, firing over the heads of the advancing soldiers. With this "preparation" the boys had been sent over the top. Some of the men were killed almost instantly, falling on top of their parapets as they were getting out of the trenches. They didn't even know what hit them. The eighty men who had arrived during the night were so green that they went over the top with full equipment, including knapsacks and blankets. They advanced en masse and thus were easy targets for the fascist machine guns. Many were killed, and those who weren't were forced to stay in no-man's-land all day. Some were killed trying to return to the trenches. Many were wounded.

There had also been many acts of heroism. On February 23, the first of the two Jarama actions, Paul Burns, a gentle Irish-American poet from Boston, had gone into no-man's-land under heavy fire and helped bring back some of the wounded. On the twenty-seventh, he had been badly wounded and was now recuperating in a hospital. Others had been killed trying to bring in the wounded.

Again I could not believe what I was hearing.

"We were told that there were only five killed and seventeen wounded that day, that you had won a great victory," I said.

"That's a lot of crap," the fellows moaned.

"Do you mean that there were hundreds of casualties?" I asked.

"Who knows? All that we know for sure is that there were only about 90 of us left. We raised a big stink about the whole action, which we felt was unnecessary and poorly organized. We demanded more training with experienced officers. But all we got was a lot of hot air."

"What was wrong with the officers? Weren't Merriman and Stember competent?" I asked.

The veterans laughed bitterly.

"That son of a bitch Stember. If he ever comes back here, we'll shoot him. On the twenty-seventh that louse was hiding in the kitchen. The next day when he came up to the lines everything was quiet and peaceful. He saw some of the boys crying their eyes out because they had lost so many of their friends. What did he do? That bastard told them they were a bunch of babies!"

We told them that Stember had spoken to us in Madrigueras and had warned us about complainers, but we hadn't understood where he was coming from. Now, our anger was explosive.

"How about Merriman?" we wanted to know.

"'Butcher' Merriman, you mean," they answered bitterly.

"What's his story?"

"He kept sending the men over the top even though he saw that it was suicide to go. If he had had any sense at all, he would have seen that it was impossible to take their trenches without our artillery, air, and tank support. But he persisted; he kept sending us over."

Charlie Nusser defended Merriman.

"Listen fellows, Merriman didn't want to send the guys over. It was

Brigade headquarters with pressure from Division that kept ordering him to keep the attack going. Merriman argued against it, but he had to obey orders."

"And Johnson . . . what about him?" we asked, somewhat confident that this time we would get a favorable answer.

Again we were disappointed. The "old-timers" thought Johnson was too high and mighty. He never spent any time with the boys in the trenches.

Despite the grumbling and the anger over the inadequate training and the lack of equipment, these men continued to fight with the Lincoln Battalion.

The next morning I was up at the crack of dawn, anxious to look this Jarama battlefront over. The trenches were no longer muddy; the rainy season was over. I noticed signs posted along different parts of the trenches with the names Marx, Lenin, and Molotov on them. Later we added Union Square, Fourteenth Street, Times Square, and more. Here, too, for the first time I heard the expression "Molotov cocktail," which were bottles filled with gasoline, a very effective weapon against tanks. The Spaniards made good use of these "Molotov cocktails" until they got hand grenades and other antitank weapons. Our rifles were Russian relics from World War I, and if you didn't keep them well oiled and clean, they would jam up and become ineffective. The Russian machine guns were also of World War I vintage, but they were in better shape.

The only nations sending aid to the Spanish Loyalists were the Soviet Union, Mexico, and Czechoslovakia, and about ninety percent of it came from the Soviet Union. I was told that Russian tanks with their crews were stationed not too far away, and now and then a Russian plane would fly overhead.

To our sorrow, shame, and yes, anger, nothing at all came from the governments of the United States, England, or France, but the people of these countries sent ambulances, food, cigarettes, and, most important, thousands of volunteers.

While in Jarama we often had the opportunity to read Spanish newspapers. I remember one day, probably in late April, reading about a "holy city" in the Basque being bombed and practically destroyed. More than sixteen hundred people were killed and almost nine hundred wounded, including nuns and priests, women and children. The city had no military significance at all and was obviously the testing ground for Hitler's new type of lightning-speed warfare—blitzkrieg.

The city was Guernica, now a household word thanks to Picasso's painting made in homage to the shattered city. At first, the Germans pointed the finger at the Spanish Loyalists. Unfortunately for the Germans, photos of the raids showed that the bombers were Heinkels and Junkers. Some days later, drunken German pilots boasted that they had participated in the raid, and finally the Nazis took responsibility.

I wrote home often in April and May, mostly to Sal, Hy, and Louise, and also to my brother, Ben. My mother didn't know I was at war, and the rest of the family back home tried diligently to keep the truth from her. Here is a sampling of those springtime letters:

> . . . The other night we had a swell time. The Italian fascists began singing songs to us from their trenches. We listened very politely. Then a number of our Spanish comrades showed them how to sing with spirit. The fascists couldn't stand it and began heavy firing. They wasted plenty of ammunition. Once in a while we broadcast to them through loudspeakers. Good results as many desert and come over to us . . . .

> . . . In this section of the front the war seems to be developing into a war of propaganda. We've been showering the fascists with leaflets for some time now and it's been very effective since many rebels have been coming over to us here.[1] Now the fascist generals, seeing how effective our leaflets are, thought they'd try the same thing on us. So yesterday morning at about five, some fascist planes appeared over our lines and instead of dropping bombs, dropped leaflets. The leaflets said that if we of the I.B. would come over to their side they would have us sent to our native countries. The paper was very soft, and very effective as toilet paper. I think they'll drop bombs from now on. . . .

. . . The other night there was a heavy shower, a thunderstorm. The fascists took advantage of it and began [an] attack. In a second all the comrades grabbed their rifles and dashed through the rain and mud for the trenches. It took less than 15 minutes to put down the attack, but what an exciting 15 minutes that was. It seemed as though all hell broke loose. . . . During all this my dugout got flooded so I spent the night in mud. Next day, though, was sunny and fixed me up.

While in the trenches, I spend much time thinking of you. I get a lonesome feeling, thinking of a nice soft bed, a chicken dinner, and the evening talks with you. Especially do I remember 11:00 PM when we hear the news of Spain. I'm usually up at 4:00 AM which is 11:00 PM your time so it is then I think of you at the radio. But I'm 100 percent satisfied. There is no place in the world I'd choose to be in now other than in the trenches. Not that I like war—I hate it, a thousand times more than ever. It's brutal, cruel, beastly, ugly—it's worse than hell—words cannot describe it. . . .

. . . I had a funny dream the other night. I dreamed that you Sal, and Hy were here in the trenches with me having a conversation on fascism. And Hy would point to the fascist lines once in a while and say, "I'm indignant." And he even took a shot at them. . . .

. . . You'd be surprised how many laughs you can get at the front. I remember one instance that keeps us laughing yet when we talk about it. The hour came to change shifts in the trench. Slim was going into the trench with his rifle and wearing only his underwear and shoes. Mike, his group leader, became very angry and asked Slim to put on his pants before going in the trench. Slim refused to do so on the grounds that it was too hot and he wanted to be comfortable. Mike threatened to arrest him if he went into the trench without his pants. Slim dared Mike to arrest him. So Mike placed him under arrest. Mike asked another comrade in his group to get his rifle and bring Slim to headquarters. So there they were, walking to headquarters, first Mike, then Slim in his underwear, and then the other comrade. Suddenly Mike remembered his own rifle was unloaded and asked the other comrade about his rifle. His too was unloaded. Only Slim's, the prisoner, was loaded. . . .[2]

. . . Another comrade tells of a rich uncle he has. This uncle owns a factory with hundreds of workers. He happens to be a communist sympathizer, so he is forever cutting his workers' pay to give money to the Party. . . .

. . . Please don't forget to tell mom I'm happy and healthy and not to worry. . . . Whenever you write, let me know about mom. If you think it best to tell her I'm working in Paris—OK. Just as long as she isn't worried. Of course, if she knows I'm in Spain, then I'm working in a factory.

. . . At night, when I'm in the trenches, a group of us get together and serenade the fascists. They evidently enjoy our singing because they stop shooting to listen. We sing everything, including peppy jazz songs, Southern folk songs, patriotic songs and revolutionary songs. There's one fascist opposite us who serenades us too. He has a beautiful voice. . . . I only wish I understood Spanish better, so as to understand the discussion going on across the trenches. It's funny to hear the fascists shout "Comrade Rojo" and the Loyalists shout "Comrade Soldado." There is no doubt that if it were possible, many more enemy soldiers would come over to us. . . .

. . . Sometimes I look around here and see the beautiful hills full of brilliant poppies and other flowers and I almost feel like crying when I realize that a war is going on around all this. And then the picture of a nice soft bed with two clean white sheets haunts me and I think of the day when I will enjoy this luxury again. And then those meals you cook—fit for a king!

And many times I just yearn for a pretty girl to put my arms around her shoulder and—but what the hell—I realize that what

I am here for is a thousand times more important than all these beautiful luxuries. If you ever saw the two little children in bandages, wounded by fascist bombs, if you ever saw a thousand people forced to live in holes of a mountain because their lives are not safe in their homes, continually being bombed, then beds and fine food and pretty girls would seem insignificant as they do to me. You feel that any amount of suffering would be worth the honor of being able to fight—yes, fight with guns, instead of words—against fascism which is so brutal and bestial as to slaughter innocent women and children with such indifference. Up to the time I came to Spain, my hatred for fascism was more or less theoretical; now it is real, the kind of hatred that makes me happy I'm here with a good rifle.

There were eight groups in our company, and each group had a sector of the trench to be covered at all hours and squads consisting of twelve men. My squad consisted of Mooch Engels, Red Bloom, Joseph Armitage, Irving Chocheles, Maynard Goldstein, Mark Rauschwald, Hy Stone, Julius Deutsch, Charlie Nusser, and a few others whose names I can't remember. Each squad was broken up into small groups of four, and these groups did round-the-clock guard duty.

One day my small group—Mark Rauschwald, Red Bloom, Irv Chocheles, and I—was in the trench doing guard duty. All of a sudden Irv called out: "Hey, look, fellows. Look at that lousy fascist. He's got his pants down and he's taking a shit."

We all looked, and sure enough, about a hundred yards away, there was a young guy "doing his duty." One of the fellows lifted his rifle to take aim, but Red pushed the rifle down.

"How the hell can you shoot a guy taking a shit in such innocence?" he demanded indignantly.

"Let's be democratic, just like at union meetings," Irv suggested. "Let's take a vote."

"OK," Red agreed. "The four of us will each mark a piece of paper with either a cross or a circle. A cross means shoot him, and a circle means let him live."

We all put our marks on pieces of paper. Red opened the four sheets, and all four had circles.

I wondered to myself if we had done the right thing. Suppose that bastard was responsible for killing our men? And yet how can you shoot a guy with his pants down? It just doesn't seem like a fair fight.

Maybe we were wrong, but deep down I believed that we "tough" communists had displayed a little fairness in battle.

About ten days after I arrived at Jarama, volunteers were requested for a special mission. It would be dangerous, we were told; we were to attack the fascist trenches that night. Ten men were needed to crawl out exactly at midnight to cut the barbed wire that fronted the fascist trenches. We new fellows felt an obligation to volunteer since the "old-timers" had already been through so much. From my group, Mooch Engels, Red Bloom, Mark Rauschwald, and I volunteered. We spent the day blacking our shoes, our faces, even our bayonets—anything that might shine in the light of a full moon. This was to be my first action, and I was more than a little apprehensive. I wondered whether I should write to Sal and other family members. But why worry them? They might get this mail and then not hear from me for weeks; certainly they would think I was killed in this action. I decided not to send any letters. I looked around and saw the other fellows writing and then destroying their letters. So we huddled together and talked about all the possibilities, each of us trying to be very brave but clearly frightened. Finally, we went off by ourselves, brooding and worrying about how it would all turn out.

At about sundown, we got welcome news; the mission had been canceled. What a relief! It was called off because all the people of Morata, a town two miles from the Jarama front, were talking about the attack that was to take place that night. Of course, the fascists must have learned about it too. That night I slept particularly well.

Occasionally we would have visitors from the States. One day, a famous novelist, Josephine Herbst, spent a few hours talking with the soldiers. After a while, she was introduced to a young Spaniard in our outfit. Herbst asked him if he spoke English.

"Sí, sí," he beamed. "Fuck you."

Herbst didn't bat an eyelash. "Your pronunciation is very good, very good."

The young soldier smiled broadly.

Another time Bob Minor, a member of the central committee of the U.S. Communist Party, visited us. We all gathered at the rear of our trenches to hear his report on domestic activities in support of Loyalist Spain. Minor, who was hard of hearing, apparently didn't hear the bullets zooming over his head. We watched transfixed as he raised his hand to emphasize some point, and thrust a finger toward the sky. We all stared at that finger, fully expecting a bullet to hit it.

Once in a while we would applaud loudly and enthusiastically. The fascists, thinking we were preparing an attack, began a barrage of machine-gun fire and lobbed some artillery over our heads. We thought the fascists were attacking, so we rushed back into the trenches. To his credit, Bob Minor asked for a rifle and was among the first to join us in the trenches.

I first met Steve Nelson at Jarama, when he came to meet the men. He was accompanied by another American communist official, Harry Haywood. Nelson was dressed in a poorly fitting, sloppy uniform, which was the typical "uniform" of the men. Haywood, on the other hand, was dressed in a shiny uniform, complete with brass buttons and expensive-looking boots, and he carried a thin stick that closely resembled a whip. Suddenly there was gunfire from the fascist lines; Haywood dropped to the ground. Nelson assured him that the bullets were way above our heads. A little while later there was more gunfire, and again Haywood dropped to the ground. The bullets were over our heads, and the area was not in any immediate danger. Needless to say, the men were not favorably impressed by Harry Haywood. Steve Nelson, on the other hand, was warmly received and was obviously well liked.

After about seven weeks in the Jarama trenches, four of us—Eli Biegelman, Joe Stoneridge, Mark Rauschwald, and I—were given a three-day pass to Madrid.

It was strange to be in this big city, to see life going on more or less normally. The hotel we stayed in had been hit by shells many times, but we felt secure and comfortable for the first time in weeks. We had a bathtub, a real toilet, and best of all, beds with sheets. However, we didn't spend our first night at the hotel; Eli, Mark, and Joe asked me to join them on a visit to a whorehouse, a first for me.

We entered the reception room and found it decorated with, of all things, huge pictures of Marx, Stalin, and Lenin. After a while, four women entered the room, all with inviting smiles on their faces. Three of them were very young and pretty. The fourth was huge, tall and fat, weighing at least 200 pounds.

Eli, Mark, and Joe immediately attached themselves to the young ones, and here I was, all 120 pounds of me, looking at this mountain of a woman.

My large friend's English wasn't too bad.

"You from the Jarama front?" she asked. "Is very bad there?"

"Yes, muy malo." I let her think that I had been through hell.

Later, when I saw all that flesh in bed with me, I had no appetite for anything. She was ghastly, like a monster. For one brief second, I wished I was back at the front.

Realizing that I was hopeless, she said, "Poor boy, too much bad war. Same thing with other soldiers from front. I know how much you suffer." Soon she was asleep and snoring. I realized that I would never get any rest there, so I quietly got dressed, left twice the number of pesetas I was supposed to, and slipped out of the room. I walked the streets of Madrid for a few hours before getting back to the hotel.

Around the middle of June, a Spanish outfit relieved us in the trenches of Jarama. My two months at the Jarama front had been relatively uneventful.

We were now sent to a small town not far from Madrid, where the newly organized Washington battalion was stationed. There I was reunited with some of my union comrades—Jerry Cook, Normie Berkowitz, Butch Entin, Hy Roseman, and Toots Fajans. Because they had just come from the States, they brought me up-to-date on our union's activities, the sit-in strikes organized by the five-and-ten-cent store workers (led by Ruth Goldstein, later to be my wife), and the organizing drives going on at Macy's, Gimbels, Bloomingdale's, and other stores.

One of our comrades, Jack Shafran, was still in jail back home, finishing a three-month sentence for his union activity. He had already volunteered to come to Spain after he was released. He, Jerry Cook, Leon Tenor (who was now at a different front in Spain), and I had been arrested so often back home, and had spent so much time in the same cell, that a prison guard had put up a sign that read: "Please keep this place clean; it is your second home." It made me feel good to be with these guys again, even though our surroundings were far from *any* of our homes.

5. Brunete

July 6, 1937, dawned bright, clear, hot, and dry. We had already marched many miles, having started an hour before sunrise. There was a feeling of excitement, of elation . . . and of apprehension. We were beginning an offensive. The Lincoln and Washington battalions were to join with units of the Spanish army and other sections of the International Brigades in an offensive aimed at the village of Brunete in an effort to break the fascist encirclement of Madrid.

As we marched along, there was nothing we could see or hear to remind us that a war was going on; birds flew blissfully overhead, sweet-scented flowers grew underfoot, and the sky was blue and clear. In the distance we could see the church spires, towering high above all other buildings.

With the Lincoln Battalion were about 250 Americans who had been through the terrible, traumatic days at Jarama; more than half of them had been wounded but had now rejoined the unit. Then there were about 40 of us who had joined the Lincolns during the last days of Jarama as replacements for the losses suffered there. The 40 of us and all those in the Washington battalion were going to see action for the first time.

My throat was dry, my canteen empty; I found myself daydreaming about sitting in a bathtub full of cold water, and then drinking the water in the tub.

The march continued; we kept on walking, hardly talking, wondering what lay ahead of us. At about noon we came to a halt. Commander

Oliver Law briefed us: "Our immediate objective is the town of Villa-nueva de la Cañada, just beyond that small hill ahead of us. At 3:00 P.M. we attack." Steve Nelson, the political commissar, told us that the main purpose of the offensive was to drive the fascists out of the Madrid area.

A few hours later, three Soviet planes flew overhead, continued over the hill in front of us, and dropped a load of bombs on the town. We heard the rumble of the bombs, saw the resulting smoke, and then heard nothing.

We lined up near the top of the hill, clutching our rifles, waiting for orders to go over the top. Suddenly, the shout: "Let's go! Let's go!" We went over the top of the hill, running forward with our rifles pointing straight ahead. Immediately we were greeted by a barrage of machine-gun and rifle fire. The whiz of the bullets went past me, and I could see men falling all around. I kept running for about another hundred yards, until the fire from the town became so heavy, there was nothing left to do but fall to the ground.

We were in a wheatfield. The ground was hard and dry. The fascist machine gunners were stationed in the church tower that overlooked the field. From their high vantage point, they could spray the entire field with bullets. I realized we were sitting ducks in the field, for although the wheat stalks were high enough to hide us, any movement stirred them and attracted immediate attention. At one point, I tried to shift my position so that I could hold my rifle more firmly. Sure enough, the movement immediately brought fire in my direction. Fortunately, nothing hit me. For hours the firing continued, never letting up. And we waited and waited, pinned down in the field, unable to move.

The wounded were moaning and crying out in pain; some were pleading for water. As the hours passed, I too became terribly thirsty; the need for water became so strong it eliminated all other thoughts and feelings. In addition, the smell of wheat was sharp and overwhelming, a smell that is still embedded in my memory.

I heard someone call out that Max Krauthamer was dead; other names of casualties were shouted over the field. Some of the wounded began to crawl back to the other side of the hill, but not many made it. I was sure we would all die, if not from gunfire, then surely from dehydration. I didn't feel much like a hero, and I didn't want to be one. I just wanted to be away from this wheatfield, away from all the suffering.

Once in a while, quiet would cover the field, but only for a minute or two, and then the whizzing of the bullets would resume. I began to think all the wrong thoughts. I tried to stop, but my mind wouldn't let me. I could be wounded in the head, in the groin, in the stomach, in the eyes. I don't want to be wounded, crippled, or killed. What the hell am I doing here? Sure, I'm an anti-fascist; sure, I want to see Franco beaten; sure, I want to help the Spanish people, but sure as hell, I'm scared. I never before knew this kind of fear; any second I could be hit, wounded, crippled, blinded, in pain, or even dead. Just like that. I guess I'm not a soldier.

I began thinking that I was in the wrong place. I wanted to do my share to try to stop the fascists, but in reality I knew I was more of a pacifist than a soldier. I couldn't kill, and I didn't want to be killed. I couldn't stand to see so much suffering and to feel so much fear. I made up my mind that if I lived through this day, I would get out of the war—even desert if I had to. I listened to the wails of the wounded. I listened to the cries for water. The sun beating down on me was torture, like being in a hot oven. So I won't be a hero, I thought. Some people might call me a coward. But what the hell do they know about war?

In the midst of all this horror, I suddenly found myself thinking again about the movie I had seen a few days before coming to Spain, *All Quiet on the Western Front*. The film had had an impact on me, and now I knew why. Now I understood the fear that the actors in that movie portrayed. So even though I believed that I was fighting a just war, that I was on the right side, the fear in me was so great, it overwhelmed my anti-fascist feelings. I had to desert. I had made the decision. I was getting out.

The hours passed slowly, and the hot sun kept beating down. I couldn't move. I couldn't spit. I couldn't sweat. I couldn't urinate. My lips were sore and cracked. I had no liquid in me except blood, and I didn't know how long I'd hold on to that. At times I thought I was losing my mind.

Suddenly I heard a voice shout, "General Miaja has sent us a message saying that Villanueva de la Cañada must be captured today!"

The words sent a shudder through me. What if an order came to attack again; what would I do?

Fortunately, no such order came. And after a short while, another voice called out, "Get back over the hill as soon as darkness falls."

What a relief! What joy! There was hope!

Unable to wait, I started back before sunset, crawling an inch at a time, clinging tightly to the earth, and then, finally, getting up and making a dash for the top of the hill and over it to safety.

There I saw many wounded, all waiting for darkness to settle in so that ambulances or trucks would be able to carry them to the rear, to hospitals. There was Charlie Nusser, my friend from Jarama, with a shoulder wound, waiting to be cared for. He had just returned from no-man's-land. He had been wounded hours before, while trying to get to a wounded comrade crying for help. I couldn't believe that he was so cheerful. "Harry, I'll be back in a week or two, as soon as this wound is taken care of. I'll miss you guys, but I'll be back."

"How can you be so cheerful Charlie?" I asked him.

"Oh, this wasn't nearly as bad as Jarama. Don't worry. I won't be away long."

I began to feel ashamed of myself. Charlie had been through so much more than I, yet he wanted to continue. I was embarrassed that I had even thought about deserting. I learned one very important lesson that day. I have never called a comrade, even a deserter, a coward. I have experienced the unspeakably horrible feeling of fear, and I realize how close I came to deserting. I know that being fearful doesn't make a person a coward. There were certainly people I thought of, and still think of, as cowards—people who blamed others for their own unwillingness to help out in one struggle or another, people who deserted from Spain and went back to the States only to turn up at HUAC hearings to testify against their ex-comrades, and one person in particular who forced a young Spanish boy, at gunpoint, to climb a hill that was being heavily shelled, while he himself remained in a safe cave.

The thought of deserting disappeared. I went through many more actions, bad ones, but never again did I think of deserting.

Our most immediate need was water; our canteens were empty, our lips parched, cracked, and painful. Rumor had it that not far from us was a river, so Hy Stone and I took off in hopes of finding it. We kept going downhill, in the direction the river was thought to be. We found the place that should have been a river; perhaps it had once been, but now it was a wide, deep, dry ditch. Hy and I decided to dig—perhaps there was water a foot or two down. So, using our spoons, we dug up the arid earth and stones, and finally came to some soft, damp earth. We put this earth in our filthy handkerchiefs and squeezed out a few drops of moisture, barely enough to even wet our lips. We gave up and headed back.

Some hours later, water, wine, and food arrived on the kitchen truck. We ate a bit, but mostly we drank and drank. I finished off a gallon of water and lots of red wine. Sleep came quickly.

The sun was hot and strong when I awoke the next morning. The order to move on was already in effect; we were to continue the advance toward Brunete. The siege of Madrid was still to be broken. Villanueva de la Cañada was only one of the towns that had to be taken before Brunete could be attacked.

Hy joined me. "How about that shelling last night!" he exclaimed.

"What shelling?"

"Aw, come on! All hell broke loose last night. Shells were landing all around us. Didn't you hear them?"

"No, it looks like I slept right through it. I didn't hear a thing. I didn't even have dreams."

"That's impossible. Look up there at all the shell holes. They were landing all around us. I got up and ran like hell. I thought you did too."

I went up near the top of the hill and looked down. Sure enough, shell holes were all over the place. I don't know how it happened, but I slept like a baby through that barrage.

"During the night," Hy explained, "Spanish Loyalist troops, together with the Lincoln, Washington, and British battalions, captured the town. Their attack caused the fascist artillery barrage."

The order came to line up; we had to move out of this position immediately. Off we went again, onto the road and through the town. There wasn't much damage in the town itself, but the road was strewn with dead bodies, mostly fascists. It was the first time I had seen dead bodies, with the exception of the few that I had seen the day before in the wheat field.

I stopped and gazed at one body, a young fascist, no more than seventeen, I guessed. He seemed so young and innocent, not what a fascist was supposed to look like. A picture of himself, his mother, father, sister, and the family dog, was sticking out of his pocket. My heart ached for him. I put the picture in my pocket. I walked on, and counted fifty more dead soldiers. All had been alive hours ago, and here they were, rotting in the sun. I wished the damn fascists would surrender so the war would end and all this killing would stop.

But, sadly, this was only the beginning. It would get worse.

Our march seemed endless. All that day and into the next morning we walked, cautiously looking for enemy snipers. At about noon we climbed a hill. In the valley below us, hundreds of men were running away; they were fascists retreating. Some ran behind trees, turned, and fired at us. But mostly they just kept running. I couldn't believe my eyes; we weren't even shooting at them.

We charged down the hill. Suddenly, we were under considerable fire from another hill just a few hundred yards away. We took cover in the ditches on each side of the road.

While we waited, one of our men suddenly began to scream. I looked at him. He hadn't been hit; there had been a lull in the gunfire. He was squirming, rubbing his face, his legs, his entire body. Several of us rushed over to him and saw that he was covered with swarming red ants, the largest ants I had ever seen in my life. They were all over him, actually eating his flesh. His face was red and bleeding, as were his limbs. We ripped off his clothing and frantically brushed off the ants. He was sent to the hospital. I often thought of him and hoped he made a full recovery.

Toward evening, after advancing through woodlands, we stopped to rest. The day had been hot and dry, and of course we were thirsty again, very thirsty, and hungry. Fortunately, the air was getting cooler, and somehow that helped a bit to diminish the need for water. Sleep overcame us.

The next morning, July 9, began as every other day at that time of year: sunny and hot.

I was now a runner for Commander Oliver Law, who had been given the command of the Lincoln Battalion during the last days of Jarama.

Law was a black man who had been in the American army for six years, but despite his obvious leadership qualities had never made it past the rank of corporal.

Law told me to call the commanders of each company together for a meeting in his dugout. About eight of us attended, including Steve Nelson, the political commissar; Paul Burns, commander of Company One; and Jerry Weinberg, another of Law's runners.

Law briefly explained what was to happen that morning. At 10:00 A.M. we were once again going over the top. Our aim was to secure Mosquito Hill, which was about three or four hundred yards ahead, and quite a bit higher than our present position. It was obvious that the enemy had the advantage. We all knew that taking the hill with our limited forces would be almost impossible.

Nevertheless, Law insisted, the men were to be told the truth: We would have to go over the top without the support of airplanes or artillery. Not a single plane, not a single round of artillery would be fired to weaken the fascist position in front of us. The simple fact was that there was not enough military equipment to cover the entire front. The only outside war materiel Spain had received was from the Soviet Union; Soviet planes, tanks, and artillery were already in action giving support to other sections of the long front attacking Brunete. We had to fight with limited arms against the massive supplies and forces sent to Franco by fascist Italy and Nazi Germany. This was the tragedy that followed us all through the war.

The meeting over, the men in the dugout began talking softly about home.

"When I get home," Law spoke wistfully, "I'm always going to sleep between clean white sheets, on a soft mattress. But first I'll drink gallons and gallons of cool water; then I'll have all the steak dinners I can eat, with plenty of mashed potatoes covered with gravy."

The others listened, smiled sadly, and nodded in agreement. Then it was time to go back to the men and mobilize for the attack.

At about 9:40 A.M., we lined up near the top of the hill. I was to be Paul Burns's runner for this action, along with John Power, a tough and wiry but small guy from Ireland. John and I stood next to Paul, who, although badly wounded earlier at Jarama, had refused to return to the States and had insisted on returning to the battalion. He was easy to like.

I watched John take a sip of water from his canteen; mine was empty.

"Can I have a sip?" I asked rather plaintively.

"Sure, go ahead," he said, and handed me the almost full canteen.

I meant only to wet my lips and throat, but somehow gulp after gulp went down. I found it impossible to stop. I emptied half the canteen.

"Gee, I'm sorry," I apologized.

"No need to apologize! I know how thirsty you are."

Another comrade saw me drinking; he asked John for just enough to wet his throat. In a minute or two, the canteen was empty. John just shrugged, and that was that. It's probably hard for people who have never known the torture of thirst to understand what it meant to give away the precious, sweet-tasting, life-saving water. From that moment on I was devoted to John Power. To me he was the greatest guy in the world.

I looked at the men around me, all waiting for the word to go over the top. These were seasoned fighters. They had been through Villanueva de la Cañada just three days ago, and they knew what we were up against. Hardly anyone was talking; everyone was staring straight ahead. I wondered what they were thinking.

Suddenly Oliver Law began running to the top of the hill. Paul Burns waved his pistol over his head and shouted, "Let's go!"

The attack had begun. I froze; I couldn't move. Maybe ten seconds passed and suddenly I was filled with shame. I was letting my comrades go into battle without me. Strangely, I forgot my fear, my thirst, my strong instinct to stay alive. I went over the top of the hill, into no-man's-land. I passed bodies that had already fallen, but I kept running for about one hundred yards, maybe more, hearing the bullets whistling around me and seeing the dust rise where the bullets hit the ground.

Then I saw John Power. He was lying on the ground, obviously in terrible pain. I fell down beside him and asked him where he was hit.

"It's my foot," he said. "Can you bandage it?"

Although he was in great pain, he spoke softly and gritted his teeth.

For the first time in my life I bandaged a wound. Meanwhile, the bullets kept hitting the ground and raising the dust around us.

"Thanks a lot, kid." John smiled weakly. "That will at least keep it clean. Man, but it hurts."

Suddenly, I was not so filled with fear. I was able to think clearly, to function. I was even ready to continue the advance. I realized that I had counteracted my fear by taking care of someone else, by being useful. I felt better.

About thirty feet in front of me, Commander Law stood up and shouted, "Let's drive them off that hill. Let's go!"

But he had no protection; he was fully exposed to the enemy. The bullets all seemed to be aimed directly at him. You could see the dust rising around him, where hundreds of bullets seemed to be converging.

John shouted to him: "Get down, get down."

It was too late. Law was hit in the stomach, and he crumpled to the ground. Jerry Weinberg, his runner, was with him. Immediately, Jerry began helping Law back, with Law crawling and Jerry dragging him. As Law passed us, he said: "It's not bad. I'll be back in a few days." He died less than an hour later. Jerry and others buried Oliver Law a short distance behind the lines; the inscription on a plain slab of wood reads: "Here lies Oliver Law, the first American Negro to command American whites in battle."

Just then word came that we were to withdraw to our original position. The attack was over. I turned to John.

"Can you help me get back?" John asked.

"Sure."

Of course, we were still in no-man's-land, with bullets flying all around. John put his arm around my shoulder, and I dragged him a few feet at a time. For about an hour we crawled slowly toward the rear. He was in terrible pain, and pulling the wounded foot over the rough terrain made the pain worse. The bullets were still flying, but not as heavily as before. Luckily, they missed us. At last we reached the top of the hill and safety.[1]

I then learned that Paul Burns had also been hit and was badly wounded. Because all company commanders had either been killed or wounded, with the exception of Sid Levine, the machine-gun company commander, Steve Nelson now became commander of the Lincolns. He asked me to be his runner and to stay close by. Then we went to the top of the hill, where our machine gunners still held their positions.

"Be on the alert," Steve told them, "but don't fire unless there is an enemy attack."

Sid Crotto and Doug Roach were piling up belts of ammunition and hand grenades, getting ready for the anticipated fascist counterattack. Their guns were still burning hot, as they had been firing over our heads at the fascist lines all through the attack. They were hoping nothing would happen at least for an hour so that their guns could cool off.

Steve spent the next few hours reorganizing the men and placing them in strategic positions near the top of the hill. Nelson was now commander and commissar of the Lincolns, and the men were delighted that he had taken over. Nelson was capable and compassionate. When the men complained about the lack of water and food, he promised he would do everything he could to get some up there as soon as possible. And the men knew he would do it. Meanwhile, Steve worried about the chances of the enemy counterattacking, and cautioned the men to keep a sharp lookout.

Much later in the day, Vincent Usera, Oliver Law's adjutant, showed up. Usera, who should have taken Oliver Law's place as commander, had disappeared; no one knew where he had been. Steve was furious.

"Where the hell have you been?" Steve shouted.

"I went to Brigade headquarters to ask for more ammo."

"You're full of shit. You were hiding. Where is the ammo, and who did you see at Brigade headquarters?"

"Uh, some officer; I don't know his name."

Steve glared at him, then turned to me.

"Harry, go to Brigade headquarters and tell Copic [commander of the Fifteenth Brigade] we are short of ammunition. Ask him to get it here as soon as possible, since we may be attacked at any time."

It took me about twenty minutes to get there, and because Copic was at one of the fronts, I gave the message to a British major, who said we would get the needed supplies that afternoon. He also volunteered the information that this was the first request for ammo from the Lincolns.[2]

On the road back there was a great deal of activity with our troops going in both directions: some wounded were being carried on stretchers, others were walking to the ambulances; other troops were going in the opposite direction toward the front. A line of tanks, returning from the front, rolled past me. They were small and surprisingly tinny-looking Russian tanks. The tankists, obviously Russians, were standing with bloodied heads poking out of their turrets.

When I got back to the battalion, I saw Hy Stone sitting on the ground staring off into space. He looked devastated and on the verge of tears.

"What's wrong, Hy?"

I got no answer.

Someone came over and whispered in my ear. "Leave him alone. He just learned that both his brothers in the Washington battalion were killed this morning at Mosquito Hill."

Hy had often spoken to me about his brothers. They were very close; all three had been raised in the Hebrew Orphan Asylum, where I too had spent some time. All along he had worried about his brothers, and now they were dead.

For the rest of the Brunete offensive, Hy hardly said a word; he functioned automatically, and not with his usual spirit. Hy was sent home after Brunete.

Down in the ditch near headquarters there were dead comrades waiting for burial. One of them was Jack Shirai, our chief cook. At first, looking down into the ditch, I didn't realize that Jack was dead. But then I saw Mel Offsink holding him, stroking his head; tears were pouring down Mel's face.

After Jarama, Jack, insisting that he had come to Spain to fight fascism, had left the kitchen and joined the infantry. Again and again, we would repeat our wishes that he would go back to the kitchen. He always laughed and told us to go to hell.

Now Jack was dead. Max Krauthamer had died instantly on July 6 when a bullet hit him in the head. Mel Offsink had lost his two best friends and, until he too was killed about a year later, was never quite the same.

July 9 had been a long, hard, bloody day. And there would still be more to get through before the day would be over. During that afternoon I accompanied Steve to the kitchen. He had not forgotten his promise to the men at the front. They were hungry and thirsty. In no uncertain terms he strongly urged the men in the kitchen to get food and liquid up to the front as soon as it was safe to do so.

At about eleven that night, I told Steve that I had to get some sleep.

"Not yet, Harry, not yet. Wait for the food truck."

When it did come, the food was lousy, the coffee cold and bitter, but the wine and water tasted good; and there was plenty of water to fill our canteens for the next day. We ate the tasteless food with gusto and drank the coffee, wine, and water.

Nelson was the last one to eat.

It was now after midnight, and I was yearning for some sleep.

"Harry, we have to go out into no-man's-land. We have to see what's there, in case we are ordered to attack again, or if the fascists launch an attack."

After alerting the posted guards, Steve and I started out. I wasn't frightened, just numb with exhaustion. I could barely keep my eyes open. I wondered how the hell Nelson could continue at this pace, never resting, always on the go, always on his feet. Nelson was almost ten years older than I, yet he had so damn much energy. It had been such a long day, and he had been on the go since early morning. He had gone over the top with the men. He had helped to take care of the wounded and to bury the dead. He had worked very hard reorganizing a decimated battalion. He had somehow gotten the kitchen to bring food up that night. All day long, he had spoken to small groups, organizing, reassuring the men, explaining, arguing, and listening with understanding and compassion. And here he was, twenty hours later, still working, worrying about tomorrow.

When the men came to him and told him they were scared, that they couldn't take any more, he consoled them, let them know it was nothing to be ashamed of, that he and all the men felt fear, or they wouldn't be human.

But here we were still out in no-man's-land. I was beginning to worry that we would still be there at dawn. At last Steve said, "OK now, let's go back."

The next day I spent a good deal of time talking with my old friend Pat Reid, perhaps the only anarchist in the battalion. We had become friends when we climbed the Pyrenees into Spain. I liked Pat despite his anarchist philosophy and his fantastic, almost unbelievable stories. Many of his stories concerned his days with the IRA. I particularly enjoyed one in which he claimed to have "organized" (a polite word for "stolen") a British army truck filled with telephone equipment. Naturally, this booty was of enormous value to his IRA comrades. The story was quite unbelievable, but it was such fun listening to him, I acted as though I believed it. And as the months went by, I liked Pat and his fantastic stories more and more.

That morning Pat commented on the lack of communications between the companies.

"Jeez, Harry, this is no way to run an army. There's absolutely no communication between companies, between battalions, or with Brigade headquarters. That's why we have to use runners; it's medieval."

Together we approached Steve Nelson. Pat told him he had gotten lots of experience in communications work while with the IRA, and that he would like to take off for a few days to see if he could get the necessary equipment for a reliable communications setup. At this time, Steve was involved in so many other problems, he only half listened to Pat. Clearly, his mind was elsewhere. But finally he said, almost absentmindedly, "OK. Go and try."

Well wouldn't you know that the next day a truck pulled up, and there was Pat in the driver's seat. The truck was full of telephone equipment and dozens of rolls of wire, tape, tools, phones—everything necessary to set up telephone communications.

"Where the hell did you get all that stuff?" I asked.

"I 'organized' it on a road near Madrid. This truck was just sitting there. The men guarding it were sound asleep in a ditch. The key was in the truck, so all I had to do was get in and drive it away. What the hell good was this stuff back there where all is quiet and peaceful? Here is where the fighting is. I'm not hurting the Spanish people. I'm helping them."

Pat gathered the people he wanted to work with him in transmissions, including Herman Bottcher, Joe Rehil, and others. Pat was appointed head of transmissions for the battalion, and his first official instruction to his men was that there was to be no saluting. He refused to become an officer. Pat Reid was a buck private to begin with, and even though he was in charge of an important group, he remained a buck private until the day he left Spain. And true to his anarchistic philosophy, he never issued orders. He would ask his men to do a job; if they couldn't, he would do it himself. If the job was dangerous, he wouldn't even ask; he'd just do it.

About a week after we started the Brunete offensive the Lincoln and Washington battalions joined forces. Both battalions had suffered heavy casualties, leaving only about 550 men to make up the new Lincoln-Washington Battalion. Mirko Markovicz was named commander of the Lincoln-Washingtons. Steve Nelson, happy to give up the command position, remained political commissar.

For a day or two after leaving Mosquito Hill, we rested and visited with each other. Many of us who had been in the labor struggles before coming to Spain—Jerry Cook, Normie Berkowitz, Butch Entin, Hy Roseman, myself, and a few others—were now in the same battalion. We had a warm reunion, exchanged stories about our battle experiences, and shared information received from friends back home about our union. I also learned, to my dismay, that Toots Fajans, another one of our union comrades, had been seriously wounded at Mosquito Hill. Weeks went by before I could visit him in the hospital. He was sent home many months later.

But our respite didn't last long. We had known that the men of the new Lincoln-Washington Battalion would be called on in the following weeks to act as shock troops—plugging up breaks in the line or reinforcing other units. And one night, just before midnight, we were awakened and told that the enemy had attacked the line at Villanueva del Pardillo. Our battalion was ordered to go to the aid of the Spaniards defending the town. Because the roads were under constant fascist air observation, we could not go by truck. We were to march quickly and quietly through a dry, rocky riverbed, and we had to arrive before dawn to avoid being discovered. The march was torturous; I was tired and sleepy, and pebbles kept finding the holes in my shoes.

Unfortunately, we did not make it before daylight, so our movement was now in full view of the enemy. Sure enough, we soon heard the rumble of approaching planes. They came in low; we were the target. Nelson's adjutant, Dennis Jordan, and I hugged the ground, flat on our stomachs. Neither of us said a word; nothing could have been heard anyway over the thunder of explosions. First there was the terrible sound of screeching bombs as they fell from the planes, then the roar of the explosions, then the hissing of pieces of shrapnel flying past us. The earth shook as though an earthquake had hit it. We were bouncing so much that we held on to the weeds and grass trying to glue ourselves to the ground. The air was so thick with dust and fumes I couldn't see a foot ahead of me. For what seemed like an eternity, the planes kept coming, one group after another.

After they had dropped all their bombs, the planes returned again, this time to strafe us. I kept thinking that surely no one else was alive, that I must be alone.

Suddenly it all stopped. When it had been quiet for a few minutes, I lifted my head and looked around. Miraculously, other heads went up also. We stood up and looked at each other. Our faces were blackened from the soot and ashes. We stared at each other, shocked and stunned by the ferocity of the attack.

Dennis asked hoarsely, "Are we still alive? Harry, were you hit?"

I couldn't find my voice. Finally, I answered: "I think I'm OK. How about you?"

"Shaking, but in one piece."

We began to move around, checking on our wounded. To our amazement, our casualties were light.

We then continued our march to the hill just ahead of us, to relieve the Spanish battalion still entrenched there. We reached the hill about fifteen minutes later and were greeted by cheers and shouts of joy from our Spanish comrades. They had witnessed the bombing and were amazed and delighted to see us come into their lines. Some of them wept, some hugged us, and some shook our hands vigorously. We all spontaneously raised clenched fists and sang "The Internationale."

Not long after we took our position on the hill, the fascist planes appeared again. This time they were much higher, so high that the planes looked like dots in the sky. We could see trails of exhaust and could hear the sound of planes in full throttle as a dogfight took place. Soviet Chatos had engaged the fascist planes in combat. We cheered and cheered. This was only one of many times that we watched Soviet planes come to our aid.

Some of the planes were shot down, and a parachutist came out of one of them. We couldn't tell whether the downed plane was Soviet or fascist. Jerry Cook, standing next to me, rifle poised and aimed toward the sky, agonized, "I can't shoot him. Suppose he's a Soviet comrade."

He didn't shoot; later we learned that the parachutist was a Spanish fascist and that he was captured by another Loyalist outfit.

A few days later we moved into a new position, a deep, dry riverbed, with a battle going on directly in front of us.

Suddenly I saw Butch Entin walking toward the headquarters staff. He greeted me with a big grin. "I got me a blighty. It's nothing. I'll be back in a few days."

A bullet had passed through his shoulder, but he clearly was in no pain. He was on his way to the first-aid station down the road, or maybe to the ambulance waiting nearby.

I never saw him again.

All our union people in Spain tried to find Butch, to learn what had happened to him. Much later we were told by John Rody, who was a first-aid man, that the first-aid station had been bombed and strafed, and the ambulance close by had also been hit. The wounded had been blown to bits. We had to assume that Butch was among the victims.[3]

Our role in the Brunete campaign was now drawing to a close. We had moved from one critical spot to another, always traveling on foot. We had very little food, water, rest, or sleep. Our clothes were ragged, almost in shreds. Our bodies were full of lice; we itched terribly. It was impossible to wash, shave, or brush our teeth. We were filthy, lousy, tired, and grouchy.

One evening, at the end of the usual hot, sunny, waterless day, the food truck finally arrived, loaded with bread, garbanzos, and wine but no water or coffee. I was so thirsty that I found myself drinking too much wine, until I was more than a little woozy. When I thought of the times I had been nearly crazy with thirst, I drank even more wine, though at the moment I was no longer thirsty.

A short time later, Nelson came over to me and said: "Harry, good news! We're being relieved and sent to the rear for a rest. A Spanish battalion is taking our place. Get word to all the company commanders to get the men ready for the march to the rear."

I started off, dead drunk and tired, trotting in whatever direction I was facing, which happened to be toward the fascists. Just before I reached the enemy lines, someone grabbed me from behind and said, "Where the hell do you think you're going? Come back with me." It was Pat Reid.

The men were already lining up, getting ready to move. Everyone was so tired. I wanted so desperately to stay in one place, to lie down and get some sleep. But we had to walk under cover of darkness, so off we went, this time on a road marked with potholes and shell holes. Pat stayed close to me. Once when we stopped for a short rest, I instantly fell asleep.

"Harry, wake up. The men are getting way ahead of us. We must catch up with them." Pat was shaking me.

"Jeez, Pat, can't we rest for just a half hour?"

"No! no! We have to be away from here before daylight. We just have to keep going. You can do it. You must do it. Now let's catch up with the men."

I got up slowly and we began the trek again. I had a splitting headache, my stomach was queasy, my feet ached, and the damned lice were eating away at me. I stumbled on in a daze, my eyes half closed, continuing only because Pat held me up and kept me going.

We were quite a distance behind the battalion, and by the time we caught up with the men, it was daylight and the sun was beginning to warm us.

Suddenly a warning cry: "Look, look! Those planes are coming at us."

There they were, nine three-motor German bombers, flying in V-formation, following the road we were on. We scattered off to the sides and fell into the fields. Everyone, that is, but Pat and me. Pat refused to run, and just leaned against the side of a barn. He refused to lie down, and, like a damn fool, I imitated his bravado.

We watched the planes, still about a half mile away and coming directly toward us. They were no more than 1,500 feet in the air, and their bomb-bay doors were already open, ready to drop their loads. Our anti-aircraft guns were firing at them, but the white puffs were missing them by a mile.

"This is going to be a rough one," Pat said softly.

We knew the bombs would be falling any second, and we were the target.

Suddenly, almost miraculously, the lead plane took a direct hit from our anti-aircraft and burst into a huge ball of fire. Everything seemed to be moving in slow motion—the burning plane, the falling pieces, the other planes separating and flying out of formation after haphazardly dropping their bombs about a hundred yards away from us. It was a welcome sight. The men began to shout and cheer. Pat, the atheist, remarked cynically, "God must be on our side today."

We continued down the road until we came to a rest area. I fell asleep immediately.

The next night Pat and I talked about the Brunete campaign. We recalled the battles we'd been through and the people we had known. One of the men we remembered was William McCuistion, a leader of the Seamen's Union. I had heard a lot about him. Everyone seemed to feel that one day he would be commander of the Americans; he was tough, capable, and brave. We misjudged him, however.

During one of the first days at Brunete, we had to cross a field under fire, so a few men at a time made the dash. When it was McCuistion's turn to run across the field, he wavered, saying that he didn't feel well. After much persuasion, he finally made the run, but when he got across the field, he kept right on running—north. That was the last we saw or heard of him, until we learned, years later, that he had appeared before the House Un-American Activities Committee in Washington, to tell of the communist role in Spain.

Pat reminded me of another incident that had taken place these past weeks. We had been resting in a field when suddenly bullets began to fly past us. There was a hill about a hundred yards away; we decided to get behind it and take up a defensive position. We began to run toward the hill, when suddenly the comrade next to me (I can't recall his name) fell flat on his face. "Have you been hit?" I asked anxiously. "No, I must have tripped," he replied. He got up and we both continued running.

A few hours later, after we had successfully stopped the fascist attack, he complained to me of an awful itch in his buttocks. He dropped his pants, and sure enough, he had been hit. There was an entrance wound, but no exit wound, so we knew the bullet was still there. He was sent to the hospital but returned to the front in a few days.

In the early thirties I had spent some time with John Rody at his parents' farm in West Allis, Wisconsin. When I first saw John in Spain, it was during the Brunete campaign, near Villanueva de la Cañada. He was leaning against a brick wall, looking pale and sick. I knew something was seriously wrong when he told me he had an awful pain in his chest. Steve Nelson, who was nearby, took one look at him and commented that he was the only pale soldier in the outfit. Nelson had him sent to a hospital where medics confirmed that he had a heart problem and suggested that he be sent home. John refused and eventually returned to the front. He became a first-aid man and proved to be one of the bravest men we had. Time and again he went out in broad daylight, risking his life, to bring in the wounded.

At the end of July the Brunete campaign was over. Our Spanish comrades, temporarily at least, had the situation in hand. The Lincoln-Washingtons were sent to Albares, a small town about fifty kilometers from Madrid, where we rested and prepared for our next action.

6. Albares

IN ALBARES WE WERE AT LAST able to shower, shave, and get a change of clothing. And, best of all, there was plenty of food and water.

At first, the townspeople were aloof, unfriendly, even nervous with our presence. They simply were not accustomed to soldiers, especially dirty, bearded, sullen-looking foreigners. It didn't help matters when three of our soldiers became drunk and frightened some of the local women. The battalion decided to punish these men by locking them up for a few days. Surprisingly, a delegation of the townspeople asked for them to be forgiven, and let us know that they understood what the men had been through at the front.

After that, our relations improved dramatically. Our doctor, Mark Strauss, was available for anyone who needed medical attention. The townspeople were grateful and delighted, because there was not a single doctor in town. Some Americans helped the peasants on their farms, while others worked with the children, teaching them American games, including baseball. It was wonderful to watch the warmth and friendship grow daily between the Americans and the Spaniards.

The most popular American was Doug Roach, a black man from Boston, who had worked for some time as a strongman in a circus back in the States. The children loved him and followed him around all day long. One day, he got under the belly of a big burro and lifted it up over his head, to the "olés" of the children and the adults, as well as Doug's comrades.

I wouldn't be surprised if it was we who introduced the game of baseball to Spain. A shipment of baseball equipment was sent by the Friends of the Abraham Lincoln Brigade, back in New York, and in Albares we had a chance to use it. We selected an area that had the best possibilities for playing baseball, but it wasn't very good. The infield was not level and was strewn with stones and rocks; trees were scattered through the outfield, and left field was about twenty feet higher than right field. Nevertheless, we played baseball, to the delight and laughter of the Spanish kids and their parents. The umpire stood behind the pitcher, and every time there was an argument—and there were plenty—the Spaniards roared with laughter.

No one wanted to be the catcher, because there was only a face mask and no chest protector. I volunteered. In fact, I volunteered for both teams. Al Tanz pitched, and he had a pretty good fastball. Everyone played with a great deal of enthusiasm, and there was plenty of shouting and arguing. About an hour and a half into the game, a foul ball hit me right in the groin. I doubled up in pain. That was the end of that game.

A few days after arriving at Albares, I was sent to a rest home on the Mediterranean along with Harry Nobel, a comrade I had known in New York. I had become very friendly with Harry during the Brunete campaign, so I was pleased that we were going together.

After a five-hour drive we arrived at a beautiful area on the Mediterranean, a place where many Internationals were resting: French, Germans, Czechs, Hungarians, British, and Yugoslavs. Harry and I were the only Americans.

The men at our rest place had lived through some of the fiercest fighting of the war, at Jarama and University City near Madrid. These were the men who had stopped Franco at the very gates of Madrid. They had been in continuous action for five or six months and had paid a terrible price. Practically everyone there had been wounded, if not physically, mentally. Many of them were missing arms, legs, or eyes.

Was it any wonder, I asked myself, that they were so quiet and seemingly aloof?

They waited here to be sent home, but the Germans, Poles, Hungarians, and Yugoslavs knew they couldn't return to their homes because of the pro-fascist governments in their countries. They were the saddest in the group.

The nights were a sharp contrast to the quiet days. We all slept—if you can call it that—in large dormitories. Every night we would be awakened by what sounded like the roar of airplanes. These sounds came from the men who were reliving their experiences in nightmares. At first, one or two of these tortured souls would begin to scream, and the screams would spread. It was frightening. Hardly a rest home.

One day I visited a nearby hospital. There was a terrible shortage of doctors and nurses; many of the wounded could not get the care and attention they needed. As I was passing one patient, he frantically beckoned me to come closer. He was on his back, obviously in great pain; he asked me to turn him on his stomach. I hesitated, not knowing the location of his wound. I looked around for a doctor or a nurse, but no one was available. The limited staff was in the operating room. I realized I had to try to help him, so very carefully I turned him onto his stomach. I was sickened at what I saw—insects and lice crawling all over his body, pus oozing from his many sores. The stench was unbearable.

Silently I cursed my government for not helping the legally elected government of Spain; at the very least, why did they not send help for the wounded? The American doctors and nurses who were in Spain were dedicated anti-fascists who came despite the many obstacles set up by the United States government.[1]

For the next few days, Harry Nobel and I made daily trips down the road to visit some of our convalescing comrades at the magnificent mansion of Juan March. March had once been thought of as the wealthiest man in Spain; he was pro-fascist and now lived in France, where he waited for Franco to achieve victory. His home had been appropriated for the recuperating wounded Loyalists who no longer required hospital care.

One of the men we visited was Toots Fajans, who had been badly wounded on July 9 when a bullet shattered a bone in his leg, causing a limp that he would have for the rest of his life. Harry and I spent many hours with Toots, gazing at the Mediterranean just outside his window. We reminisced about our union days back in New York; we exchanged the latest news received by mail from Clarina Michelson, president of our union, and from an organizer named Ruth Goldstein.

Paul Burns was also there. He was anxious to return to the front but couldn't get permission because of a serious wound, his second one. John Power was another "guest" who was impatient to get back to the front. He hoped to fully recover in another month. John showed me a letter he had just received from his girlfriend in Ireland, telling him to give "Harry Fisher, the Jewish lad from Brooklyn, a kiss" for helping John back to the rear when he was wounded.

The days spent at the Juan March home were really pleasant. It was good to be with our friends, and there was plenty of good food and drink.

Going back each night to our "rest home" was another story.

Walking on the road in the dark was eerie. Every farm or house had vicious dogs guarding the property. They pranced onto the road, staying close at our heels, snarling, growling, and scaring the hell out of us, until we were well past their territory. We didn't dare pause or turn around for fear we would be torn to pieces. Even the heavy sticks we carried gave us small comfort. This went on for the full hour it took us to get home. We followed this routine for three nights and then decided we'd had enough. We rejoined our battalion at Albares.

At Albares the food was plentiful and superior to that which we had had at the front. We ate all our meals in the local church. Everyone helped himself to generous portions from huge pots placed on a long table.

One day there was a large bowl of salad, a luxury and rarity during our stay in Spain. Carl Bradley, a husky seaman from Baltimore, stinking drunk, began to mix the salad with his dirty hands.

"Take your lousy hands out of the salad," I shouted at him.

Bradley glared at me, his lips tightened, and his face turned red and ugly. Without saying a word, he picked up a large kitchen knife and started toward me. I was too surprised and shocked to even move. Mooch Engels was a few feet away, leaning on his rifle and quietly watching Bradley's moves. As Bradley lunged at me, Mooch picked up his rifle and hit Bradley over his head. Still frozen in my tracks, I heard the thud and saw Bradley go down. He was out cold, and we thought he was dead. But a few minutes later he stirred, and some of the men carried him to his bunk where he slept it off. The next day Bradley came over to me, very abject and apologetic. He insisted that he didn't remember anything. He put out his hand and we shook. I can't say that we became great friends, but I sure was careful with him, especially if he had been drinking. He was also one of our best and bravest soldiers, honored many times for his heroic and daring actions, not including his attempt on my life.

In early September, the battalion went back into action, this time in Aragon, a string of towns called Quinto, Belchite, and Zaragoza. Our objective was to capture a well-fortified fascist position near Quinto.

I missed this action because Steve Nelson, then Brigade commissar, asked me to take his car to Barcelona for repairs. Barcelona was beautiful and peaceful at that time. During the day I walked and sat on benches along the Mediterranean. At night I slept in the car in the repair shop, just to make sure that it wasn't "organized."

When I returned to the front, I was very upset to hear a horrifying story from Pat Reid. We had captured over four hundred prisoners during the battle for Quinto, he told me. The fascist soldiers were mostly very young men who seemed relieved and happy that they had been captured and had lived through the battle. But one young soldier, a looie, was the only one to keep his officer's stripes in view after his capture, obviously very proud of his role. Pat was one of the few Americans informed that this young lieutenant would be executed by a firing squad. Pat was indignant and decided to speak to Steve Nelson to try to get him to stop the execution. According to Pat, Steve was not happy about the task of killing a prisoner, but someone higher up, most likely in Brigade, ordered him to have one officer executed, because the fascists had been killing any International, officer or not, who was captured. Pat argued that this prisoner could not hurt anyone now, and that we should not lower ourselves to the level of the fascists. He argued that if the fascists killed children, we wouldn't imitate them and kill children as well!

It seems that when he was told he was going to be executed, the soldier shouted pro-fascist slogans such as "arriba España" and "viva Franco." The execution took place away from most of the battalion. Pat witnessed it with tears in his eyes. He told me the names of those on the firing squad, but I quickly—and intentionally—forgot them.

7. Belchite

BY THE TIME I RETURNED to the front, the battle for Quinto was over. Now our objective was to capture Belchite, an important stronghold of the fascists, a town that controlled many strategic roads.

Taking Belchite was not going to be an easy task; the city was well fortified, and the fascists, who received their supplies by airplane drop, were determined to hold it at all costs. Along with Spanish brigades and other International battalions, the Lincoln-Washingtons fought on for about a month. The battle for Belchite was difficult, involving hand-to-hand fighting, bayonet attacks, house-to-house searches, and street fighting.

At that time I was assigned to transmissions, which was part of the headquarters staff. One day out in the field just outside of Belchite, I suddenly saw bombers closing in. I hit the ground. The bombs began falling, and once again I found myself wondering if I'd survive. Then, suddenly, here comes Harry Hakim, crawling around the field, distributing the mail. He brought me a big pack of letters, the first mail I had received in about six weeks. As the bombs fell, and as the earth shook, I kept thinking about those letters. There are few things so precious as mail during wartime, especially when you are at the front. Will I survive the bombing? I wondered. Will I be able to read my letters? At last! The bombing was over and I was in one piece. I hurried off by myself to read and reread those precious letters from home. I must have read them a hundred times. There was one from my mother that made me laugh.

Oliver Law, third from right, leading an attack at Villanueva de la Cañada,
July 6, 1937. He was killed three days later at Mosquito Hill. Photograph by
Sam Walters.

Front row, left to right: Bienvenido Domingue (Cuba), Jack Schulman, Joe
Azar, Julius Deutsch; back row, left to right: Joe Stone, Morrie Teitelbaum,
Sam Stone, Robert Zimmer, John Murra. Both Stone brothers, members of
the Washington Battalion, were killed at Mosquito Hill, July 9, 1937.

Burial of Jack Shirai, near Mosquito Hill, ca. July 11–12, 1937. Photograph by Sam Walters.

Harry Fisher with David
McKelvey White, Albares,
August 1937. Photograph by
Sam Walters.

Mark Rauschwald was an artist who carried his painting materials with him through Spain. Here, he is painting outside his tent, after the battle of Brunete, summer 1937. Photograph by Sam Walters.

The family of a fascist soldier who was killed July 7, 1937, at Villanueva de la Cañada.

Oliver Law teaching use of machine gun to two comrades at Jarama, spring 1937.

Left to right: John Power (Ireland), unknown Canadian, Harry Hakim, Irv ("Toots") Fajans. Photograph by Sam Walters.

From left: Max Krauthamer, Eli Biegelman, Mel Offsink, Jarama, spring 1937.
Krauthamer was killed July 6, 1937, at Villanueva de la Cañada; Offsink was
killed in March, 1938, during the Retreats.

From left: Irv Chocheles, Harry Fisher (reading), Charlie Nusser (in front of
Harry), Hy Stone (on right at water tap); Jarama, spring 1937.

Front row, left to right: Unknown, unknown, Dave ("Mooch") Engels, Joseph Armitage (Canada), Dave Weiss, John Oscar ("Red") Bloom (Canada). Back row, 3rd from left is Irv Chocheles; others unknown. Jarama, spring 1937.

Maynard Goldstein, Jarama, spring 1937. Photograph by Sam Walters.

July 23 1938
Dear Son:

I received today the letter you wrote April 15.

I am very glad to hear from you, but I'd be happier to see you. Don't be angry if I don't write more often. About three weeks ago Sal wanted me to write to you, but I told her to wait because I thought I'd have a lot of news to write you. But it didn't turn out the way I thought it would. Ben [my brother] took a maidl out and I thought something would come of it. Nothing did. I hope you come home and marry before Ben. In fact, there's a maidl I want you to meet.[1]

There isn't much work now. Maybe about two days a week. I have more time to worry about you.

Now let's talk business. I want you to come home.

You always listened to me. Listen to me now!

I just made new raspberry jelly. I remember how you used to lick it when you were here. Wasn't it good? If you want to fight fascism, you can fight it here. You meet it at every step—more than in Spain. In a pencil factory on 14th Street, lots of pickets were arrested. I almost expected to see your name among them.

If you want to have pleasure, come home and look at Louise [my niece]. You won't believe your eyes. If she comes into a room, you don't have to put the lights on. I went to see her dance recital. I'll never forget it. She got so much applause, you'd think she was a famous actress. This was the first time in my life I had such a good time. The next time will be when you come home.

There were 20,000 people in Madison Square Garden last Tuesday at a meeting to raise money for Spain. What speakers! A priest spoke and said Russia was the only land that was godly. A good collection was taken.

I got two letters from Poland this week. They ask about you. I wrote them that you were in Spain. They want me to bring my sister's son to America. I went to make an application and I was told that I must have five or six thousand dollars to post as bond. If I don't have it, I can't make out the application. In their letter they ask me to ask my brother to post the money. What a case! He would never do it! Pinkie still comes every Sunday. He davens for you; he prays that you come home in good health. Maybe it will help. Just come home.

If Bennie were in Spain, he'd make a quick job of cleaning up the fascists. He's very thorough. He went after the cockroaches this morning. He never misses one. Ben is in a good mood today. I woke him up to tell him there was a letter from you. He jumped out of bed.

All my friends in the shop read your letters. They are anxious to get news of you. I promised them a grand party when you get home.

Mrs. Schiff's son, I don't know his name, comes to me every Saturday to find out if I've heard from you. I bought Sal a fur coat for her birthday. I'll buy us a house when you get home. Come home!

I gave a donation to the Friends this week and I gave Sal money to buy you cigarettes.

Regards from everyone. I want to see you soon.

Lovingly,
Your Mother

So much for keeping my whereabouts secret!

The next day was quiet in Belchite; there was a lull in the battle. A group of us, including Jerry Cook, Jack Shafran, Normie Berkowitz, Hy Roseman, and some others, were sitting on a street curb just outside of town when a truckload of items sent by the Friends of the Abraham Lincoln Brigade arrived from the States.

Large boxes of cornflakes and powdered milk were distributed. After having my fill of this extraordinarily delicious treat, I stuffed my pockets with more cornflakes and saved them to nibble on later.

We also got corn on the cob, another luxury. When the Spaniards saw us eating it, they said we were crazy, that corn was animal feed. We couldn't get them to try it. But they did try some of the rolls of toilet paper we received. They'd never seen toilet paper and, thinking it was writing paper, used it to write letters to their families.

The next day the order came to try to capture a building in the center of town. Captain Lenny Lamb gave the order to Mooch Engels, explaining that the fascists were holed up in this building, sniping at the Americans. Mooch and his squad were told to flush the fascists out of the building, not an easy task. He took his squad of twelve men armed with rifles, hand grenades, and one machine gun, and opened fire on the building. The noise was terrific. The trouble was that Mooch had attacked the wrong building—the fascists were in the building behind him. But the racket he and his men created was so deafening and scary that it frightened the fascists who began waving white flags from the windows behind Mooch and his squad—but they didn't see them and kept right on attacking.

"¡Aquí, aquí!" the fascists yelled, intentionally drawing attention to themselves. The Americans turned around, realized what was happening, and ordered them out of the building. The fascists seemed relieved to comply.

The next day, Dave Doran, who was now Battalion commissar (Steve Nelson had been wounded the day before), brought a truck with a loudspeaker into the town. Someone shouted over the loudspeaker in Spanish for the fascists holding the town to surrender, to leave the town with their arms held high. He advised them that they would be treated according to the international rules regarding prisoners of war.

After a while, a lone soldier appeared with his hands over his head. He conferred with Dave Doran, then went back in to the town. There was about a half hour's wait, and then a line of hundreds of fascists began their march out of Belchite, dropping their rifles in a pile and keeping their hands over their heads. They looked pathetic—skinny, drawn, and frightened; they repeatedly asked for "agua, agua."

In one group, there were five nuns who had worked in the hospital taking care of the sick and injured. They came out with the walking wounded, many of whom had to be helped by other soldiers. Dr. Strauss approached the nuns, and gave them bandages, medicine, water, and cigarettes to be distributed to the wounded. Some of the nuns burst into tears, surprised and relieved that not only were they not going to be shot, but that they were being treated decently. When the nuns brought the supplies to the prisoners, they were shocked and amazed.

As the fascists were being loaded onto trucks to be taken to the rear, one of them asked: "Rusos, are you Russians?"

"No, Americans, de los Estados Unidos."

He shouted to the other prisoners, telling them that the United States was in the war on the side of the communists!

Steve Nelson had been wounded just before we took Belchite. As usual, he had been up front at a position closest to the fascists. He had refused to take adequate cover. His wound, located just below his stomach, proved to be very painful. Dr. Strauss got him to his car and drove him a few miles to the front-line hospital, where the wounded were first taken for immediate attention before being sent to the better-equipped hospitals at the rear.

A few days later, Dr. Strauss and I went to visit Steve. On the way, Dr. Strauss explained the seriousness of Steve's wound. I was very upset and barely spoke a word during the trip. Dr. Strauss was equally moved and kept brushing tears from his face.

We arrived at the hospital and had to wait awhile before seeing Steve. The wounded lay on the floors in the hallways, bloody and filthy, waiting their turn to get a bed and attention. The doctors and nurses moved silently about, their faces drawn, lined, expressionless. They were unable to show their feelings; they were so weary, utterly exhausted, and yet they forced themselves to continue to care for the wounded, to carry on with the operations. This went on day in and day out. Only when someone died would a wounded man in the hallway be carried in to occupy the now empty bed.

At last we did get to Steve's bedside. He was optimistic about his wound, didn't think it was too serious. He was sure he would be back at the front in a few weeks. While talking to us I noticed his eyes flicker across the aisle. Very quietly and sadly he told us that the Spanish soldier in that bed had had both his legs amputated that morning. The soldier was unaware of it, still under the effects of anesthesia. We were with Steve about an hour later when the now-conscious soldier lifted his blanket and saw that he was legless. He wailed a heartbreaking scream.

A nurse rushed to him but could not console him. Another patient, next to Steve, called out to her. He was in terrible pain. She turned from the Spanish soldier, squeezing his hand sympathetically. She then went to the patient near Steve. She was so exhausted, emotionally and physically, that as she bent over this patient, she simply fainted. A passing doctor tried to rouse her but finally shrugged his shoulders and said, "Let her rest."

Steve did return to the battalion a few weeks later, but only to say goodbye to the men. He had been asked to return to the States. Bob Minor, who was the representative of the Central Committee of the U.S. Communist Party to the International Brigades, was with Steve.

The men were both sad and happy when they learned that Steve was leaving the battalion—sad at the thought of losing him, but happy because he would now be safe. Even Pat Reid, the cynical anarchist, had only praise for Steve.

At that time the policy was to send home those men who had been at the front for at least six months. I fit into that category. Dave Doran, who had replaced Steve Nelson as the Lincoln commissar, came to see me a few days later. Dave was a red-cheeked, handsome, American boy-next-door type but was not as popular with the men as Steve had been.

"Harry," he said, "you've been through all the battles during your six months here, so we're sending you home. And before you leave, we'll commission you a lieutenant."

I was a little taken aback at this news and said, "Great! But why am I getting this promotion now?"

"It will make a better impression back home when you speak at meetings about Spain. As a lieutenant, your words will carry more weight."

"Sorry Dave, but I've been a buck private all the time I've been here, and I'd rather go back as a buck private."

Doran sighed. "Well, it's your decision, but I think you're making a mistake."

Obviously, Pat Reid had had an influence on me. He had steadfastly refused to be commissioned an officer, and I knew that, like him, I could never give orders, especially if it meant sending a soldier on a dangerous mission. I remained a private until I left Spain a year later.

8. Tarazona

AFTER A FEW DAYS, I was sent to Tarazona, the new American training base. It was a little town, very much like the one in which I had trained before going to Jarama. Tarazona was the arrival area as well as the departure point for Americans.

Being away from the front gave me a chance to write home about events in greater detail.

October 3
Dear Sal, Hy, and Louise:

I finally received Hy's fine letter written Sept. 2. I read it while my nerves were a bit tense, because of what happened during the day, and it quieted my nerves down a bit.

Here is what happened yesterday that upset me. Irving, I and a few other fellows were spending the afternoon in a small pleas-ant town on the coast. Suddenly everybody was looking up in the sky, and sure enough—four huge bombers were roaring by. Just as they got near the town, they dropped some of their bombs. So once again, I heard that familiar, terrifying hiss of falling bombs, and then the nerve-wracking explosions, even though most of the bombs fell in the water.

But what shook me up was the effect of the bombing on the women and children. As soon as the bombs began falling, women and children began crying and yelling and ran about aimlessly. Irv, I and the other fellows tried to calm them and get them to lie where they were. The planes came back a second

time, seven of them. This time Irv and I were with a seven year
old boy and a middle-aged man. The boy was trembling and sobbing. He couldn't understand what it was all about. I tried to
calm him by saying, "es nada"—(it's nothing). But I noticed I
was nervous myself. When the sound of the bombs hissing
downward came, the boy lost all control of his nerves and shook
like a leaf in a gale. It was pitiful. The planes came back a third
time and dropped bombs. By now the whole population was ter-
rified. I don't think any damage was done, but it sure scared the
people. After it was over, I saw a group of women and children
come out of a tunnel with water knee deep. They were all wet
and most of them were sobbing hysterically.

And talk about Spanish pride! The middle-aged man who fell
next to us was very ashamed to lie on his stomach in a street in
such an undignified way. When he got up, he explained he was
doing this for the sake of his mother, as his death would hurt her.

Last night I began to think how awful it all was. Yet this was
nothing as compared to Bilbao and Guernica. What brutal agony those people must have gone through—those who lived
through it. This incident brings home clearly the methods of fascism—terrorizing women and children.

Can you also imagine how much torture the civilians of Canton
went through when Japanese bombers did their job? We here in
Spain follow the events of China with just as much concern as the
events in Spain. I watched some wounded comrades read about the
bombing of Canton and their faces expressed both horror and anger. Just imagine what the next world war will be like.

Another fellow from the Department Store Union is here with
us. He was wounded at Quinto and is here to recuperate. His
name is Morty. I don't think you know him. We haven't heard
from Leon for some time, but a doctor tells us that he saw him
recently in good shape driving an ambulance on the Cordova
front. So the only one we have to worry about now is Butch.[1]

Love,
Salud,
Harry

It was now early autumn, and the weather was cold and rainy. The area was full of mud and slush. There were about two hundred newly arrived Americans still in training and about ten of us waiting to be sent home. The ten of us slept on the cement floor of the school building, in a long corridor with doors in front and back. There was a continuous draft, and mud covered the entire floor. The toilet was a large ditch in the yard out back. I was covered with lice and for months had been suffering from constant itching and scratching; I had sores all over my body. I had no energy, no appetite; my body ached; my mind was fuzzy. Three times a day, we'd slosh through the mud and rain to another building where some slop was put into our mess kits. After eating—or trying to eat—we'd walk back to the school, lie down on the hard, cold floor, and wrap ourselves in blankets. Two or three days passed. I felt sicker than I ever had in my life. I couldn't even make it to the mess house. I just stayed put on the floor, shivering one minute and then sweating and burning. Someone, I think Jack Corrigan, brought some soup and water to me once or twice a day; if he hadn't, I probably would have starved to death. In addition, I had a bad case of diarrhea. During the worst days, I'd have to get up every ten or fifteen minutes, put on my boots, and go out in the rain to the ditch. The mud was so thick and deep that soon my boots were filled with wet mud—so I began to go out barefooted. Even my two blankets were now muddy and wet, but they were all I had.

One day, Captain Allan Johnson, who was in charge of training the new Americans, came in to see us. All the men in the room stood up at attention, except me. I stayed on the floor, too miserable to give a damn about anything. I felt his boot nudge me, and I heard his command: "Get up and stand at attention when an officer enters."

"Fuck you," I whispered.

"Who is this soldier?" I heard Johnson ask.

Someone replied, "He's been here for a few days, waiting to go home; he was at the front for more than six months. He's ill, and he just lies there without bothering to go for food."

Johnson left, ignoring me completely. To this day, I cannot understand why he didn't send me to the hospital in Tarazona.

After some days I began to feel better, and although I had no appetite, I went to the mess hall at last. My choices were garbanzos or grapes. Without too much thought, I grabbed a bunch of grapes and coffee. What a mistake! In no time I was back at the ditch.

A few days later, John Murra showed up. John was working in Albacete, about twenty-five miles from Tarazona, in the office that housed all the records concerning the Americans in Spain—those at the front, those in training, those who had been wounded, and those few in jail. Among other responsibilities, his job was to make sure all the U.S. volunteers got their fair share of the weekly rations. He took one look at me and said: "What's happened to you? You look like a skeleton! I thought you were on your way home!"

"I've been sick and I'm still waiting to be sent home."

"Well, while you're waiting, I have a job for you. It will be pretty easy, and it will give you a chance to regain some strength. We have just received a tremendous shipment of goods sent by the Friends of the Lincoln Brigade in the United States, and I would like you and Jack Corrigan to guard it."

We found Jack, and the three of us went to the gymnasium in the school building. There, stacked from floor to ceiling, were cartons of cigarettes, chocolates, toilet paper, canned food, and many other precious items. John was honest as the day is long and wanted to make sure that our "luxuries" didn't fall into the wrong hands. He instructed us that no one was to take anything without a note from him, and that meant absolutely no one, including the officers.

I was happy to be in a dry and draft-free place. I placed two benches together and made that my bed. It was quite comfortable after the damp, muddy floor I had been sleeping on.

Jack and I had one rifle between us but no bullets, a fact that only we knew. I got to know Jack really well during the time we were on this guard detail, but his reputation had preceded him. He was the fellow who had climbed the Eternal Light flagpole at Madison Square Park back in New York and had raised the "Free Ernst Thaelmann" banner.

One day, Captain Johnson came to the gymnasium and asked for a few cartons of cigarettes and a carton of chocolate.

"Do you have a note from John Murra?" asked Jack.

"No, I don't need a note from Murra. I'm the commander of this base."

"Sorry, you can't have anything without a note from Murra." Jack was firm.

Johnson, ignoring us, headed for the cigarettes. Corrigan pointed the empty rifle at him and said quietly: "Hold it right there!"

"What the hell are you doing? Put down that rifle or I'll have you arrested."

But he didn't take another step forward. He saw the determined look on Jack's face and quickly left the gymnasium. Jack sure had a lot of guts.[2]

Captain Johnson, who had been in the U.S. Army, was determined to bring military discipline to the Americans at Tarazona. He issued an order that all officers were to be saluted and that any American who passed the Spanish flag in the town square must salute that flag—and smartly. Some of the soldiers obeyed the order, but there were those who refused to salute anybody or anything. Johnson, outraged at this violation of his order, called a meeting of all the Americans and demanded that his order be carried out. All those who refused to do so would be placed under arrest.

One American volunteer, unaccustomed to this kind of military discipline, asked innocently, "How close to the flag must we be before it becomes necessary to salute?"

"Within thirty feet!" Johnson answered imperiously.

And again, innocently, "How will we know when we are within thirty feet?"

"We will paint a circle thirty feet around the flag. When you step inside the circle, you will salute!"

Accordingly, a circle was painted around the flag.

The Spanish people in the square watched with great amusement as the Americans walked the line, somewhat like drunken sailors, trying not to step inside, sometimes stumbling into the circle, giving a quick salute and getting back in line again. It became such a farce that the whole affair was stopped after two days.

One day, the entire base was told to report to the church after dinner, to hear a report by Bob Minor on the world situation. I kind of admired Minor, who came from Texas, because before becoming a Communist Party functionary he had been a cartoonist, and a damned good one. I still remember seeing one of his cartoons in the *Daily Worker*, showing an American at an army recruiting station. The recruit was naked from the waist up, with a tremendous physique, muscles bulging. But he had no head. The general in charge was looking him over, a balloon caption containing his thoughts: "The perfect soldier."

Captain Johnson had learned that I had been arrested with Minor once back in New York, during a department store strike; we had spent half a day together in a jail cell. Before we gathered in the church, Johnson said that he would like to introduce me to the crowd first so that I could tell the story of our arrest and then introduce Minor. I agreed.

The church had been stripped of all its benches, and the fellows were sitting on the floor. The lighting was poor; about a dozen candles were scattered around. Johnson stood at the front of the room, but he forgot to introduce me and went directly to Minor. Just as well, I thought. I wasn't one for public speaking.

Minor spoke in a booming voice, giving us descriptions of various world events, touching on one country and then another . . . for more than two hours. No one listened. When Minor would pause, I could hear snoring—which apparently Minor, who was hard of hearing, did not notice. On and on he went.

At long last he was finished and left the church to a smattering of applause. The fellows were getting up and stretching, grateful that the talk was over. But Johnson ordered them to sit down. "We have one more speaker," he announced. I wondered who the stupid jerk could be who would continue this torture. I could hardly believe it when I heard my name called out. Now I knew who the stupid jerk was. I slowly made my way to the front, to the mutters of the disgusted audience. I turned and looked at them, and their angry faces glared back at me. All except Johnson's. He expected a dramatic jailhouse story.

What the hell can I say to these guys, I wondered. I stood for a few seconds, took a breath, and gave the best speech of my life: "Enough!" I said in a loud voice, and headed straight for the door.

The applause was deafening. There were whistles and "bravos." I'm still proud of that speech.

In early November, word came that I was to join John Murra in Albacete, to act as his assistant until it was time for me to go home. John and I became very close during those few weeks in Albacete. One day, he told me that he was very troubled about a run-in he had had with an American soldier named Alex Pratt.

Pratt had come to John's office to get his weekly ration of cigarettes and chocolate. He had been drinking, was in an ugly mood, and demanded extra rations. John had refused. Pratt cursed John, calling him a "rear-guard coward" and accusing him of letting others fight while he lived like a king. Of course, these were ridiculous charges. John was a great guy, principled, objective, and brilliant. He was fluent in Spanish, French, German, Italian, Russian, and English, along with his native Romanian, and was naturally in great demand at various International Brigade locations whenever a translator was needed. Everyone knew that the work he was doing was critically important, and that he was anything but a coward. Nonetheless, Pratt's thoughtless and cruel words affected him. "I'm going to find a way to get to the front," John told me.

I tried to tell him that he was needed right where he was. I also wanted him to know that Pratt was not someone whose words should be taken to heart. I remembered an incident involving Pratt and a company clerk named Owen Appleton. A member of the YCL and the son of the president of a Boston bank, Appleton was a quiet, scholarly young man. It was his job to dish out the few pesetas we volunteers were paid each month—perhaps the equivalent of two or three dollars. One day Pratt complained loudly that he should be getting more pesetas. He became abusive and demanded more money from Appleton, who listened quietly and then said, "Your pay *is* too little. I don't need any money. You can have mine."[3]

John listened to my story and said, "Yes, but Appleton is at the front. I've been in Spain nine months, and I've never been to the front. Maybe I am a coward, like Pratt said." But John was no coward, as would become obvious to everyone during the Ebro offensive. Pratt, the real coward, was the person I would later see holding a pistol to a young Spaniard's head, forcing him to climb a hill that was under attack, while he himself remained safe within the walls of a cave.

In late November, the Albacete office underwent major changes. Bill Lawrence, who had been the commissar of the base office, had been sent home, and John Murra, his assistant, was reassigned to the International Brigade headquarters in Barcelona. John Gates was arriving from the southern front to take over the Albacete office. Murra recommended that I be named Gates's secretary, and for about a month the three of us worked together in Albacete, Murra showing us the ropes.

John Gates was well known in American progressive circles, first as a student leader, then as head of the Communist Party in Ohio. He proved to be a complex character and not an easy man to like. He was not kind or compassionate like John Murra. He rarely smiled.

On November 30, 1937, I wrote home:

Dear kids:

You can see by the typing that I'm working in an office. It's a very tough job, keeping me on the go from morning till night, but something I like a lot. I never knew I could be so happy and busy at the same time. I'm being broken in as the secretary of the American Commissar at the base, here in Albacete. It's a very important job held during the past seven months by a young student from the University of Chicago. This comrade is getting another important job, and I'll soon be taking his place. Meanwhile I'm working with him. The only handicap I have is that I don't speak all the languages that are spoken here. John, the young student, speaks French, German and most of the others as well. All I speak besides English is a bit of Spanish. Anyways I think I'll get along and at the same time I'll be learning more of the languages.

Gosh, if you only knew how much I missed you during the days I was resting after being taken out of the front. I was quite

weak for a while, for about two weeks, finding if very difficult
even to walk. I spent most of those days in bed on the Mediterranean coast, and began thinking of all the old days, and how
much fun we used to have. Then I took stock of everything,
whether it was worth my while to have come to Spain and
whether it did me any good. I can assure you that it didn't take
me long to find the answer. Nothing has awakened me to the extent that my stay here in Spain has. I'm convinced that I want to
stay in the revolutionary struggle for the rest of my life. The
thing is so clear and simple here. There are two sides to it and the
fascists are always facing you. Do you remember Hy, how we
used to talk of the day that we would be behind barricades, how
political differences would disappear, that democrat, socialist
and communists would fight shoulder to shoulder. I remember
that last day in Belchite, while we were building a new barricade
on a street corner that I smiled to myself. When we had those
discussions, they were only theoretical. I never thought that
someday I would be behind barricades. It wasn't theory anymore. It was practice. It was real.

Don't think that I feel that war is glorious. I'm not Mussolini's
son. It is impossible for anyone to go through this war without
being a real hater of war in the future. You have no idea how
ugly and brutal it all is. I've seen strong comrades go crazy almost—and seeing a strong comrade weaken is heartbreaking.
It's much worse than seeing one die. There is one British comrade, a damn good fellow, who had a bomb drop twenty yards
from him. He got a bad case of shell-shock or something so that
he can hardly walk. He can't move his head. He's a pitiful sight
to look at. Yet I remember him just a few months ago, big,
happy, strong. You can imagine how I feel when I see him now.
What is surprising about this case is that the comrade's brain is
normal and that he is sorry only because he can't be of much
more use.

I bought a pair of those things you drum with in your hands as
you do the Spanish tango—castanets, I think you call them—for
Louise. If it is possible, I'll mail them. Otherwise, I'll have to

wait till I can take them home. I know Louise will be an excellent dancer by the time I get home. I'm looking forward to seeing her dance. It might not be a bad idea for Louise to teach me how to dance, so I can lead a normal social life.

Regards,

love and salud,

Harry

While John and I were in Albacete, we often visited the wounded in a nearby hospital. One day, on leaving the hospital, we saw a nurse assisting Bob Colodny, the same fellow who used to come into our cabin on the *Ile de France* and throw the bull with us.

At Mosquito Hill, he had been hit in the head by a bullet; a comrade pulled him in from no-man's-land. Everyone thought he was dead, but the first-aid man heard his heart beat and quickly got him to an ambulance. He was still in a coma when he arrived at the hospital; he was not expected to live. The doctors did not give up and worked with him every day. After seven or eight days he came out of the coma. And here he was on the streets of Albacete learning to walk again. His walking wasn't too bad, except when he stepped off the sidewalk into the street, or when he tried to get back on the sidewalk. Still, he refused to let the nurse hold his arm; he wanted to do it himself. The nurse stayed close to him, ready to catch him if he faltered. It would take twenty seconds or more for him to step off the sidewalk and even longer to get back up. His determination and courage were tremendous.

When he finally got back to the States, he earned his B.A., M.A., and Ph.D. degrees in history at the University of California, Berkeley, and he eventually became a professor of history at the University of Pittsburgh. During the McCarthy period of the 1950s there were repeated attempts to have him expelled from the university for his leftist beliefs and for his fighting in Spain. The harassment went on for years, but he continued teaching until he retired in 1984. He is the author of one of the best books on Spain, *The Struggle for Madrid.*

Toward the end of December, Gates and Murra received instructions to close the Albacete office. Murra was to take all documents and records concerning the Americans to the headquarters of the International Brigades in Barcelona, where he was being reassigned. Now I had to make a decision, whether to return to the front or to go home to the States.

Just about this time, the Spanish Loyalist Army captured Teruel, a tremendous victory for the Spanish people. The enthusiasm was unrestrained and very evident all over Loyalist Spain.

I decided to return to the battalion. I was in good health now, and I wanted to be with my comrades. I was happy to have come to that decision, even though I knew that the war was far from over and that the Loyalists had very little chance of winning.

9. Teruel

GATES LEFT IMMEDIATELY to join the Lincoln Battalion; he became commissar of the Fifteenth Brigade, which included, besides the American battalion, the British, Canadian, and one Spanish battalion.

In Murra's Albacete office, there was a closet filled with cartons of cigarettes and chocolates. We had to dispense with all of it before closing the office. Murra decided that most of it should go to the hospital in Albacete and the rest to the front. Several of us who were headed for the front filled our knapsacks with the cigarettes and chocolate, stuffing every pocket, and then carrying more packages by hand. On the morning of the last day of 1937, we boarded a truck with all our goodies, and off we went, headed for the front.

Later that morning, we stopped to pick up a comrade I had known very well in New York, Joe Byrnes. Joe had earned a reputation as a bureaucrat, but I liked him in spite of his bossy ways. He was friendly, charming, courageous, and generally well-meaning.

"It's good to see you, Harry," Joe greeted me. He told me that things were popping in the States, that Spain was on everyone's mind. He brought me up-to-date about friends back home.

"We heard about what was going on here, and I was sent by the party to straighten things out, to take hold of the battalion," Joe told me.

"What do you mean?"

"You know what I mean, the demoralization of the fellows in the battalion. We were told that things are terrible, that there's no spirit, that everyone is low, with no fight left in them."

"That's crazy," I said. I was shocked that Byrnes thought he could take over the battalion after it had existed for more than ten months.

"Joe, I've been in the rear for three months now, but I know something of what's going on, certainly more than you do. You say that the men are bitching and complaining—well, that's true, but it's true of any soldier in any army who has been through as much warfare as we have. I was one of the loudest bitchers, but I'm going back to the front, even though I could be going home. And, I expect to do a lot more bitching. But when we are at the front, our spirit is good. The men will do anything asked of them. In the rear, we all blow off steam, gripe, and complain. If you tell them you're going to take over, they'll raise all kinds of hell, and then you'll really see some griping. After all, some of them have been through six months and more of fighting, some as much as ten months. They've been through the fire, and they are the ones who should take over. When Steve Nelson came, the men had very little experience, but it's different now."

None of this convinced Byrnes.

Later that day we arrived at Aguasvivas, a little town about thirty miles south of Teruel.

I immediately reported to Dave Doran, the political commissar. He asked me to be his runner, but I told him I wanted to work with Pat Reid in transmissions. Dave reluctantly agreed.

It was great to see Pat again. He threw his arms around me and said, "Harry, now I can tell my stories to someone who appreciates them."

Then I was greeted by Normie Berkowitz, Jerry Cook, Jack Shafran, John Rody, and many, many others. I felt as though I were home again. I was very happy to be with these guys.

"Hey, Harry," Pat said, "you came at the right time. We're going to have a good party tonight, a real New Year's Eve party. A pig is already being roasted and we have lots of wine. It's going to be great."

"Well, I have a contribution to make." I turned over dozens of cartons of cigarettes and chocolate that Murra had given me. Pat's eyes opened wide when he saw all the loot. He thought we should share it, so we gave half to Company Three, John Rody's company. Then Pat gathered the transmissions men and distributed our share equally. Because I didn't smoke, I gave my cigarettes to friends in other outfits.

Unfortunately, our plans had to be shelved. An hour before the party was to begin, we got word that the front line in Teruel was cracking and that the Internationals were being sent there immediately. To add to our dismay, the weather had taken a turn for the worse. The temperature had plummeted to twenty degrees below zero; a heavy snow was falling, and strong, icy winds buffeted the area. We climbed into open trucks, and a long convoy formed behind us. I rode with Pat and Marty Sullivan. In the middle of our truck was a large garbage can with wood burning in it. We tried to get warm by putting our hands close to the fire and jumping up and down on the moving truck. Nothing helped. We were freezing; our hands were numb, our faces turning blue. Every ten or fifteen minutes the convoy would stop; we would get off the trucks and run up and down the road, but even this didn't help.

At last, near midnight, we reached our destination, a flat area surrounded by hills. Some of the men were assigned to guard duty. I was lucky. The transmissions unit, to which I now belonged, was able to take shelter in a barn. It was still cold, but at least there was no wind or snow to contend with inside. I gathered up a pile of hay and lay down, exhausted. The mice and rats scurried around and over our bodies, but we knew we were better off than the men doing guard duty. Indeed, the next day some men were rushed to hospitals with frostbite.

The battle to keep control of Teruel was intense; we were bombed daily. It was at this front that the enemy used a new weapon, a shell that exploded in the air blanketing the area with shrapnel. The shelling was bad enough, but when the shells exploded above us, we'd have to run every which way for cover. Our casualties were extremely heavy.

I had a relatively soft job at the Teruel front manning a switchboard located at the foot of a hill, about a mile from Teruel. A first-aid station was set up in the same area. The wounded were brought here until ambulances took them to hospitals. I spent much of my time trying to help the wounded.

Teruel was a rough front for most Americans. The transmissions unit didn't suffer too much, except for Pat Reid, who never asked for volunteers and always did the most difficult jobs himself.

Marty Sullivan often visited me at the switchboard. He brought me news of friends who were in more dangerous positions. Sully was a wonderful man, a good comrade, a courageous soldier, a loyal friend. Unfortunately, he was a heavy drinker, but to his credit, he drank only while he was at the rear, never at the front.[1]

The commander of the battalion at this time was Phil Detro, a tall, good-looking Texan, a Democrat, and an admirer of President Roosevelt. Respected and well liked by everyone, he was one of the few non-communists who rose to the rank of commander of the Americans. Some of the fellows used to kid Detro good-naturedly, asking him how he could be an admirer of President Roosevelt, because Roosevelt was not allowing U.S. aid to the Loyalists. Nonetheless, he got along wonderfully with all of us. When Sully told me that Detro had been wounded, I felt terrible. He died two weeks later in a hospital.

The next day Sully, Pat, and I went into the city of Teruel, which was still in Loyalist hands. There was much less damage than I had expected, mainly because it had been so cold that for some days the fascist planes couldn't take off, and even artillery pieces had frozen and couldn't be used.

The three of us went into a big restaurant in Teruel, closed now because there were hardly any civilians there. We went into the basement, which was as large as a gymnasium. There, stuck in little cubicles all around, were thousands of bottles of wine. About a dozen Americans were also sitting around a large tin with a fire going, trying to keep warm.

This was going to be a cleaning-up interlude. We all stripped to the waist, began pulling lice off our clothes and our bodies, squeezing them between our nails until we heard a little crack, and then throwing them into the fire. We lice-killers each had a bottle of wine. We drank, killed lice, and told stories. It certainly would have seemed bizarre to an uninitiated observer, but we were relaxed and actually having a good time.

I was drinking something that was sweet and thick, but before too long, I was woozy, so I stopped. Sully also was getting giddy. Pat told him to lay off, that he'd be going back into the lines soon. Sully put the bottle away and didn't touch it again.

One day, toward the end of the month, I was in a big, open space on top of a hill. It was still cold, but at least forty degrees above what it had been when we first arrived. I decided to break the ice in a nearby frozen body of water to wash and shave. The shaving was more like plucking hairs off my face, and all of it done without mirrors or soap.

Some reporters arrived to interview us. For the moment everything was peaceful. One reporter, a man from the Jewish communist paper *Freiheit,* was talking to me when we saw a group of nine planes in the distance. We realized at once that they were German planes, flying low, and coming directly toward us. The interview was cut short, and the two of us flopped down on our stomachs on that hard, cold ground.

We heard the whistling and screeching, and then the loud explosions of the bombs. The earth shook, the dust rose, the horrible odor of gunpowder filled our nostrils. Fortunately, the bombing was over in minutes, and the planes turned around and disappeared. Surprisingly, we had few casualties.

The reporter was frightened and admitted that it had been a terrifying experience; he was leaving immediately. He stopped to ask me how I could take it. I shrugged my shoulders; you can't go through a bombing and not be scared.

The battle for Teruel, with its cold temperature and horrible bombings and shellings, was now over. We had suffered numerous casualties. Teruel was once again in the hands of the fascists.

We were withdrawn from Teruel early in February. My outfit boarded trucks with all our equipment and headed for a position in the rear. The rest of the outfit boarded freight trains. We then met in a small, hilly town near Segura de los Baños and took shelter in the homes of local peasants. Sully, Pat, and I went to stay the night in an elderly couple's old house. The couple was warm and friendly and tried to give us food, but at the moment we had more than we needed. We gave them some of our food and cigarettes, and in the morning we boarded our trucks. The rest of the men got on their freight train. The next day we joined up in an open field and dug trenches, just in case any bombers should appear.

One day, I was sitting on a hill with Pat and several other comrades when a few small fascist planes appeared in the distance. Moments later they were overhead and began bombing the valley below us. The whole incident took only a few minutes, the planes leaving in a hurry as several of our rifles and one anti-aircraft gun quickly opened fire on them. Suddenly, scores of comrades came rushing out of a bomb-damaged barn, some of them almost naked from bomb blasts that had torn off much of their clothing. I remember a few men on the hill laughing at what seemed to be a comical sight, not realizing that the men running from the barn had been hurt.

Pat and I quickly took off down the hill to see if we could help. We were separated, and I found myself on a dirt road. Some distance in front of me was a badly wounded American with blood gushing from his thigh. With him was a small, unimpressive-looking soldier by the name of Joe Luftig, desperately trying to apply a tourniquet to the wounded soldier's leg. Suddenly, a single plane reappeared, flying at perhaps 100 feet above the ground; the pilot was throwing small bombs or hand grenades out the window, aiming at the three of us on this exposed road. As the low-flying plane got closer, the pilot began strafing the road with machine-gun fire. My instinct was to make a dash to shelter, but when I saw Joe ignoring the plane, devoting his attention to the wounded comrade, I had to join him. I rushed over to the two of them, bullets splattering all around us, but just watched as Joe finished setting the tourniquet. I don't know who the wounded soldier was, but he surely owed his life to Joe's courage.

We remained for a few weeks at this "rest" area. It was February, and we were beginning to feel the welcome warmth of the sun in the daytime— the sensation that comes with spring, no matter where you are, that life is renewed. There was an inner surging of hope as well as the security of being some miles from the front.

We were fortunate in that the food truck came regularly. On February 12, Lincoln's birthday, we had two hard-boiled eggs apiece in honor of our namesake. This was such a rare treat that I spent an hour slowly nibbling at this delicacy.

Bull sessions were now in full force. I joined one group but just sat and listened. They were talking about an incident involving Earl Browder, secretary-general of the U.S. Communist Party. A group had been on a freight train heading for the rear. Suddenly the train had stopped. The passengers were taken off the train and brought a few hundred yards into the woods, where they were greeted by Earl Browder. He gave a report on what was going on back home, but he ended his speech with a dire warning. He told these men, who had just endured a month of hard and bitter fighting, had suffered many casualties, and had survived cold and hunger, that he had heard that there were some grumblers among them. He sternly announced that anyone who grumbled or complained would be taken out of the battalion and sent home as punishment. The men were stunned, hurt, and angry. Especially so were the seamen, who had been excellent soldiers and good communists and were ready to do anything to defeat the fascists. The meeting ended with some of the men saying facetiously, "I'm grumbling, I'm grumbling—when do I go home?"[2]

I had been in Spain for one year now, and, sadly, there was still no end to the war in sight. The fascists were much stronger than we and had far more planes, artillery, tanks, and manpower. Interestingly, the morale of our troops was excellent, and this in spite of the fact that the fascists had recaptured Teruel.

Although the daytime was warm, the nights were cold, very cold, but I was exhausted after the long, freezing winter, and I slept well, not only at night, but also during part of the day.

One day, Jack Corrigan and I asked for permission to spend the day in the auto park, some miles away, where many of our friends were stationed. Someone gave us a lift in a car, and we had a great day. Our friends dined us as though we were heroes, even though they had also gone through hell and had suffered their share of casualties driving their trucks to and from the front.

I spent some time that day with Ralph Fasanella, the young Italian-American who had shared the cabin on the *Ile de France* with John Murra and me. Today, critics call Fasanella one of the best artists in the United States. In those days he had not yet realized what an enormous hidden talent he had.

Later that day Corrigan and I decided it was time to return to our battalion; one of the men volunteered to drive us back. When we arrived back at camp, we were surprised to see the battalion gone. Obviously, they had moved suddenly, and there was no one around to tell us where they had gone. So here we were, two lost soldiers, not knowing where to go or what to do. Just then an ambulance drove up, and the driver informed us that he was headed for the battalion. We climbed onto the roof of the ambulance, sat on some mattresses, and held on for dear life as we bounced along the rough, curving, hilly roads. But the time passed quickly, and I enjoyed talking with Corrigan.

That was the last time I saw him. He was killed a few days later, on March 10, the first day of the retreats.[3]

We reached the battalion in a few hours, where we set up camp within sight of Belchite, a city we had helped capture about six months earlier. We knew we were near the front, because we could hear the not-so-distant rumble of artillery, and there were scores of German planes flying overhead daily. In spite of that, we felt relatively safe. Vladimir Copic, the commander of the Fifteenth Brigade, was on leave. Both Lenny Lamb, commander of the Lincolns, and Milt Wolff, Lamb's adjutant, also were on leave. Evidently, they had believed that things would be quiet for a while. Dave Reiss, a courageous but inexperienced soldier and commander of the machine-gun company, had been made temporary commander of the Lincolns.

Two days after we arrived at our camp outside of Belchite, the fascists dropped English-language leaflets in our sector boasting that they were about to begin their offensive and demanding that we surrender, telling us we would be spared and sent back to our families. This meant the fascists knew where we were and how many of us there were. Their intelligence must have been pretty good.

On the morning of March 9, I was awakened by the distant sound of planes dropping bombs on nearby villages. All morning, the rumbling of the artillery became louder, and the fascist planes became more numerous. It was obvious that the fascist offensive had begun. By afternoon, the artillery rumble had gotten much closer, and we suspected that the enemy had broken our lines and were advancing. For a while we had felt secure in this position, but now that feeling of security was evaporating. We knew we'd soon be in the fight once again. All the fellows had that same strained look on their faces that could be seen each time we prepared for action.

We waited and watched the skies. Sometime that day, we saw three planes circling over Belchite, about a mile away. Suddenly, one plane started to dive almost straight down. We thought it had been hit and began cheering, but after almost reaching the ground, it dropped its load and started to climb again. The second and third planes did the same thing. We were baffled, having never seen anything like this. Later we read in the Spanish newspapers that the Germans had tried something new in warfare, dive-bombing. Belchite was a testing ground for World War II, where the Germans used dive-bombing on a large scale. That day we were witness to the Germans' first practice sessions.

That afternoon, Harry Hakim went to Brigade headquarters, which was located on the other side of Belchite, about two miles away. When he came back, he told us that the civilians were packing their belongings onto wagons and carts and beginning an exodus, moving toward the Ebro River. A short while later, the order came to stand by, to be ready to move at a moment's notice. We knew we'd be moving to the front very soon, this time to try to stem the fascist advance.

I spent that evening with another New Yorker, Sid Rosenblatt, and Yale Stuart. Sid was battalion clerk and a close friend of the temporary battalion commander, Dave Reiss. Yale was chief of the observation group. The three of us sat up until midnight, expecting to move at any moment. Finally, in sheer exhaustion, we all dozed off.

10. Retreats

MARCH 10, 1938, 3:00 A.M. YALE STUART was waking us, shouting: "The front has been broken, and the fascists are close to Belchite. We've been ordered to close the gap. Our orders are to move immediately to the front."

The words "we're moving to the front" always had the same effect on me. My mouth would dry up, and butterflies would play havoc with my stomach. The thought "Will I make it this time?" kept running through my mind.

Someone's voice was raised in anger not far away. Bob Merriman, from Brigade, was yelling at Dave Reiss, saying, "You're supposed to be on a hill two miles from here. I sent a runner to you at ten last night with that order. Why the hell are you still here?" I had never heard Merriman so angry. He was usually very calm and composed, but today he was in bad temper, unshaven, and wearing filthy clothes. He bawled the hell out of Dave—who would be dead in about seven hours. Dave meekly tried to explain that he never had gotten a message the night before.

In fifteen minutes our battalion was on the road. The night was dark and quiet, the fear so strong it was like a nightmare. The road was full of refugees fleeing the front. They moved silently, carrying only the few possessions they could take with them, some carrying little babies. Most were women, and there were some children and older men. They plodded along, heads down, moving as though they were being drawn by a mighty magnet. Obviously, this was not the first time they had fled the front. They were so sad, so tired. It was heartbreaking to see such suffering. It made me forget my own fears. Soon all the civilians passed us, and we were alone on the road.

Somehow, for the moment, everything was peaceful and, yes, even beautiful. The sun was just starting to rise, and the sky glowed with soft, luminous colors.

I was walking at the head of the column, near Commander Reiss. Sid Rosenblatt and I had a casual conversation with Reiss as we walked. Everything seemed peaceful, and we didn't seem to be in any imminent danger.

Reiss was philosophical. "This is crazy," he said. "The only thing I had to do with war before this were the antiwar demonstrations I took part in back home. I was a pacifist, and in a way I still am. Yet here I am, commanding an American battalion, made up mostly of antiwar demonstrators, looking to take on the most experienced fighting force in the world today. What a crazy world."

As the sun came up, Reiss halted the column; he had noticed movement on the hill just ahead of us. Not knowing who was there, Reiss decided to send scouts ahead. Sully and I lay down together and closed our eyes. Moments later bullets began flying over our heads. "Get behind those hills," Reiss shouted. A few men had been hit, but none seriously. Sully and I stayed down, flat on our stomachs for a while, and then began walking quickly toward the hills behind us. When we heard more bullets whiz by, too close for comfort, we lost some of our dignity and did some fancy running.

Just as I got to the back of the hill, some shells landed close by. I jumped into a shallow ditch and almost landed on Leon Tenor. He grinned at me and said, "Welcome to my new home." Leon had been one of the leaders of the Ohrbach's and Mays department store strikes. We had been arrested on the picket line many times and had become good friends back in New York. This was Leon's first experience since joining the Lincolns after being an ambulance driver on the southern front for a while.

There was a lot of excitement going on to our right. Planes appeared overhead, bombs began to fall, and more and more fascist artillery opened up. We saw soldiers in the open field running backward a few feet, dropping down, and firing their rifles in the direction of the fascists. We learned later that they were from the British battalion, scrambling back toward Belchite, away from the fascist onslaught—just as we would be doing in a short time. These were the first hours of a retreat that lasted four weeks and ended when we reached and crossed the Ebro, which was still in Loyalist hands. The march through enemy territory began with about five hundred Americans and two hundred Spaniards. Many of us lost contact with our companies and had to get through the fascist lines in small groups and sometimes even individually.

"Leon, I better get on that hill and find headquarters and see what's cookin'. I'll see you later."

I didn't see Leon until some years later. He was one of many Americans to be captured within the next few hours.

I found headquarters a few minutes later in a huge cave that was divided into many "rooms." This was the Hermitage of El Puego, three miles west of Belchite on the Fuentetodos road. Present were Dave Reiss, Commissar DeWitt Parker, Marty Sullivan, Sid Rosenblatt, Yale Stuart, Al Prago, and about twenty others. Everything seemed calm in this cave. It seemed to be the safest place in the world. No bombs or shells could land in there. The inside of the cave was similar to a church. There were electric lights, many rooms, religious pictures hanging on the "walls," and some good furniture. I felt secure and safe, but not for long.

Dave Reiss kept trying to get Brigade headquarters on the phone. Finally, utterly frustrated, he turned to Sully and me and said: "You've got to go out and repair the lines. I must talk to Brigade." My heart sank. No doubt about it, I was scared. Sid Rosenblatt looked up at me and whispered, "Good luck."

Sully and I left that haven and picked up the telephone line that led to Belchite. We found the first break in a short time and repaired it, but we still could not get Brigade to answer, so we started for the next break. Within half an hour we had repaired five breaks, but now we couldn't reach either brigade or battalion headquarters, which meant there were new breaks behind as well as ahead of us, obviously caused by the heavy shelling going on at the time. Sully and I soon realized how hopeless our task was, as shells were landing all around us. The line wasn't only broken here and there. It was completely smashed.

More planes appeared overhead, so we took shelter in a viaduct under the road. Sully and I didn't say much. We'd both been in situations like this before. We watched as a single plane came very low and chased one soldier. Every time the soldier fell, we were sure he'd been hit, but soon he would get up and start running again. The plane turned and followed him again, shooting at him all the time. At last the plane left, and the soldier got up and began walking. We watched in amazement as the soldier strolled nonchalantly down the road, as though what had happened was a routine thing in his daily life. To me and Sully, it was a big victory. We felt like cheering.

Just then, we saw someone running down the road from the hills we had left half an hour earlier. It was Yale Stuart. He had a bandage around his head with a splotch of red in the front. He was frantic, couldn't speak, and kept pointing desperately toward the hills. We knew something terrible had happened. Finally, the words burst from his lips: "They're all dead up there, the whole headquarters staff—Reiss, Parker, everyone. We thought all was clear, and we came out of the cave just as a bomb or a shell landed. Oh my god, you couldn't recognize anyone. There were heads, legs, hands, flesh, blood all around. It's horrible. No one's alive but me. I can't stand it. I'm getting to Brigade." And then he was off, sprinting down the road to Belchite. Sully and I looked at each other. We were both shaking.[1]

We looked toward the hills. Hundreds of troops, American and Spanish, were running on the lower part of the hill, headed toward some thick woods that might offer protection. Nine enemy planes in single file were diving, one at a time, at the fleeing troops. Their guns kept splashing bullets all around the soldiers. And behind the running men were more than a dozen tanks also shooting at them.

"Jesus Christ," yelled Sully. "They're being slaughtered. They haven't got a chance." Two single planes were strafing one soldier who was running in our direction. He was hit just a few hundred yards from us. He stumbled and fell, and we knew he was finished. I was sick to my stomach. My knees felt like they had turned to water. The dirty bastards!

During the Ethiopian war, Mussolini's son, a fighter pilot, had boasted to the Italian press about the defenseless civilians he had strafed. It was like duck hunting, he had said. And now I watched as two planes chased one soldier and effortlessly shot him down. I could picture the pilots grinning as they struck their prey.

Sully and I saw another column of men, some Spanish and some British, marching to our left. We raced over and joined them, moving into some wooded ground where we could not be seen from the air. We kept moving to the rear, through the shelter of the trees. A Spanish lieutenant was in charge. We were cool, disciplined, and orderly. Most of the men had rifles, and we had a few machine guns. We walked for about two hours, picking up more and more men, until we had a column of about one hundred.

We could still hear the rumble of war behind us, sometimes not so far behind. Finally we came to a fortified hill, not too far from Belchite. It was an anti-aircraft and artillery position, but all the guns had been removed and taken to the rear. When we reached this fortified position on the hill, many others were already there. Besides Sully and me, there were only a handful of Americans, about fifty British, and the rest Spanish, all in all about three hundred men, including many wounded. The officers held a meeting, and we could tell there was disagreement among them. Some believed we should stay and put up a defense line right there, while others thought it would be best to get away while it was still possible. Finally, the decision was made to stay and defend the hill.

Sully and I were given rifles and put on guard duty. Later we were given cans of condensed milk. I never tasted anything quite so good. It was the last food we had for the next day or two.

While Sully and I were on guard duty, we saw a group of some twenty soldiers walking toward the hill, all of them carrying rifles. We called out a warning to our Spanish lieutenant.

"¡Manos arriba!" shouted the lieutenant. Some of the soldiers dropped their rifles and raised their hands. Others raised their hands but held their rifles over their heads. To everyone's delight, they proved to be Loyalists; they joined our ranks on the hill.

It was now late afternoon; the war seemed to be quieting down. But looking toward the fascist side, we could see lots of movement, all headed in our direction. Although no more planes were in the sky and the artillery was quiet—even the small-arms fire had ceased—the fascists were moving up, consolidating their gains, and getting ready for the next day. The view from our hill was excellent.

With the darkness came cooler air and a sight that amazed us. Hundreds, perhaps thousands of small bonfires were lit in the fields on three sides of us. Brazenly and without fear, the enemy had built fires to warm themselves and to heat their food. It looked like a tremendous picnic.[2]

A rumor spread that we were surrounded by the enemy, that sooner or later we would have to fight our way through their lines. But right then, Sully and I could think only of sleep. At about eleven o'clock that night, we were relieved of our guard duty, and in a short time we were both sound asleep.

At two o'clock in the morning we were awakened and told that we would have to get through a small break in the fascist line. We had to move in a hurry, before dawn broke, or it would be too late. No smoking, no talking, no noise at all. We learned later that some of our men had been sent out the evening before to guard one particular road situated behind the hill we had occupied. The fascists evidently had decided to wait for daylight before completing their encirclement of the hill. We walked very slowly, because we had many wounded with us. Some were carried on stretchers, some on the backs of comrades; some were able to walk. The going was tough and slow, the only sounds being the groans of our very badly wounded.

At dawn, we were still moving away from the fascists, but we had made it through their lines and now were relatively safe. Some of our soldiers with machine guns were positioned alongside the road, waiting for us to get through, before joining our rear. Sullivan and I and about ten others were ordered to stay about a hundred yards behind the machine gunners, to act as a backup to them. Our instructions were to stay until the machine gunners left their positions, at which point we were to catch up with our retreating troops, which we did.

About an hour later, two trucks arrived for the wounded, and thereafter the rest of us were able to move on foot at a faster pace. Before noon, at a crossroads, we encountered a group of almost a hundred Americans and Spaniards from the Lincolns; John Gates was in charge. Sullivan and I and some others from the Lincoln Battalion were told to stay with Gates, while the rest of the men went on to join up with their own battalions.

Although only about thirty hours had passed since the retreat had started, the men, tired and hungry, were anxious to put up a line to prevent a fascist breakthrough in this sector. Sullivan and I were stationed behind a stone wall that separated two farms and faced the crossroads. For a few hours everything was calm, although once in a while we could see fascist planes flying overhead.

Late in the afternoon, about eighteen German three-motor Junkers, flying quite low at about three thousand feet, headed straight for us. We knew we were in trouble. Sully looked at me and said, "Here we go again!" We saw the bombs leave the planes like little glistening raindrops, a beautiful but frightening sight. We hit the earth fast. I realized that we were in a lousy spot, right near this stone wall, a wall made up of huge rocks that could easily bury us in a few seconds. But it was too late to move. And then came the now-familiar crashing, screaming bombs hurtling through the atmosphere, sounding like shrill whistles and howling cats; then the ear-shattering explosions, the cloud of dust, the dryness in the mouth, and again the fear that perhaps I was the only one to survive.

Then from Sullivan: "Are you all right, Harry?" and I knew that I was not alone. Only two men had been killed, but some had been badly wounded.

After dusk, we were on the move again. This time we came to a wooded section in the hills, where we were told to get some rest. Some men on guard duty formed a circle around the camp, and every two hours the guards were changed.

As usual the night was quiet, although now and then we did hear a plane flying nearby. I had no idea what was going on, where we were, or what we would do next. I knew I was hungry, but there was no food. Fortunately, we had been able to fill our canteens with water, so we didn't have to suffer the awful thirst that we had during the Brunete campaign.

I was sitting next to John Gates on a hill, about a hundred feet above the road. Suddenly, we saw men running on the road below us. They were fleeing a tank that had just come into our view—a German tank, almost directly below us.

"Goddamn it," groaned Gates. "We have to get the hell away from here before they cut us off. Harry, get to each company commander, and tell them that we are moving now, right now. Don't mention the German tanks. Just tell them to get the men together and follow me."

Before I left Gates, I looked down; now there were four German tanks.

The men mobilized quickly, and we marched away from the road. We came out of the woods and into open fields. Now we had to worry about the skies above us. But we just kept going. Bill Mayer was with me at the time, and between us we carried a heavy case of ammunition. Some fellows were lugging heavy machine guns. Once in a while, we would see fascist planes in the distance—undoubtedly scout planes—and we'd be ordered to get down and wait until the planes were out of sight.

The day was March 12, my birthday. I wondered if I would live through the day. Bill and I talked about New York while we carried that heavy ammunition box; we swapped stories about what we would do when we got back home. Eventually we reached a road where some Americans, also in retreat, told us where we could join up with the Lincoln Battalion.

Normie Berkowitz, also in transmissions, caught up with me when we came to a hill that the Lincolns were defending. At the foot of the hill stood Jim Ruskin, who was in charge of transmissions for the Fifteenth Brigade. He was from England, an engineer, an intellectual, and what we called a "one hundred percenter." A devoted Communist Party member who never deviated an inch from the party position, he was a stickler for discipline, for saluting, and for neatness when possible. He would never waste a morsel of food, insisting that we too eat every scrap. But he was courageous and fair, well liked and highly respected.

Ruskin used to listen with keen displeasure when Normie and I bitched. He misunderstood our bitching to mean that we were disgruntled soldiers and would desert at the first opportunity. He was, therefore, surprised and happy to see us come off the road. He not only shook our hands with great enthusiasm, but he hugged us and said, with a big smile on his face, "I never thought I'd see you two again. I thought that by now you'd be in France. God, but I'm proud of you. Look, you're even carrying rifles."[3]

Ruskin then told me that because we didn't know just how long we would be in this position, there was no need for transmissions. He suggested that the transmissions group join up with another outfit of the Fifteenth Brigade. Because we weren't sure where the other outfits of the Fifteenth Brigade were, Normie, Sully, and I joined an infantry group. There we were given positions and told to dig. We used spoons and bare hands, digging and scraping, until we made a dent in the hard ground where we could put our bodies in case of more shellings or bombings. I managed to get a few hours of sleep that night in my foxhole, but I was on guard duty for the rest of the night.

There was no food, except for a little dried bread, but at least we felt safe—we were with a large unit of perhaps three hundred or more men, and we even had two of our tanks on the hill.

A letter home expressed my thoughts:

Hello kids:

My hands are cold and I can't get stationery—so accept this note for the time.

It's been raining plenty—so the war has stopped for the time being. We're in a reserve position—taking life easy.

Even tho I haven't been writing lately, I want you all to know I haven't forgotten you—in fact I've been thinking of you more than ever. I miss you terribly. Dream about being with you every night.

Now about things here. Just a few impressions. The other night we marched 20 kilometers to a new reserve position. We were tired and cold when we reached our destination. Three of us entered a house and fell asleep on the floor. I was worried about what the owner would say in the morning. When I awoke, I noticed that we were covered with blankets. The people in the house put them over us during the night. In the morning they brought us wine and nuts. It made me feel good to see this comradeship between soldiers and civilians.

Our soldiers are singing again. All over our camps—there is singing. Can such soldiers ever be licked? I'm sure that the Italians didn't sing last March after their defeat. One time during the retreats everyone was blue. The fascists were in front of us and behind us. A little group began singing. Before you knew it, hundreds were singing. This cheered everyone up. Things didn't look so bad. Surrounded and retreating soldiers singing. How the hell can they be licked.

The next afternoon, a small plane came directly toward us, flying at under one thousand feet. Obviously, it was a scout plane, and we knew that when it returned to its base there would be many other planes coming to bomb us. Our orders were to shoot at the plane, actually to shoot in front of it. Then as it came over us, it began to leave a trail of smoke, and we all cheered, sure that we had hit it. It disappeared over a hill, and we just hoped that we had actually brought it down.

Then, suddenly, we saw a fascist cavalry attack one of our hills, no more than a mile from us. We watched the whole action; it was unreal, awesome, and terrible. The two tanks on our hill, as well as artillery or tanks from our other hills, began lobbing shells in the horsemen's direction. We could hear the firing of machine guns and rifles. We saw many of the horses stumble and fall and men who had obviously been hit fall off their horses. The fascists were losing this battle and clearly had suffered serious losses. Soon they retreated to their base positions, but in fifteen minutes they made another attempt to attack. They did not succeed, and they once again retreated to their base positions, this time to stay.

The men on our hill felt relief and a sense of hope after watching the fascist cavalry take a beating. Then, to add to our good fortune, a kitchen truck arrived with bread and coffee, which was immediately distributed to the hungry men.

That afternoon, John Gates, once again Brigade commissar, stood in the center of the hill and brought us up-to-date on events taking place around the world. A cheer went up when he told us that the question of aid to the Spanish Republic was just then being discussed at a meeting of the League of Nations.

By evening things were once again "normal." We were told that we would have to move again; the fascists had us almost encircled. So once more we mobilized and marched all night, going through fields and wooded country. All I could think of was sleep and food.

We finally came to a place just outside of Caspe. We were told that we were going to set up our lines here and defend the town. The fascists were very close, and although we weren't sure of their numbers or exactly where they were, we knew the bulk of their forces were on the high hills surrounding Caspe; we also knew they had tanks and lots of artillery and planes. On the other hand, we had only rifles (Russian) and some machine guns (World War I vintage). We had no artillery or air cover.

I was again working with transmissions. We had gotten some new men, and the battalion was a bit stronger but still only half of its original size.

We spent about three days in this position. Some of our men were stationed on the north side of Caspe, with Milt Wolff as commander in charge; the rest of us were in the woods just west of the town.

On the third day at this location, I spotted Lou Cohen sitting and staring at the ground. Lou and I had been active in the YCL in 1933 on the Lower East Side of New York City, which at the time was one of the most poverty-stricken sections in the country. And now, four years later, here was Lou in Spain!

"Lou!" I shouted with glee. "When did you get here? How are you? Gee, it's great to see you!"

Strangely, Lou ignored my greeting. His eyes were riveted on the ground. He wouldn't look at me.

I tried again. "Lou, are you all right? Can I do anything for you?"

He remained silent, still staring at the ground.

I didn't know what to make of it, but I decided to leave him alone for a while. I patted his shoulder and left.

About an hour later Lou approached me, held out his hand, and apologized for his behavior. Then he explained. He had been in the square the evening before, and what he had witnessed just about broke his heart.

"About thirty of us were with Wolff," he said, "and we reached the square in Caspe without any trouble. Suddenly, a tank came from around the corner, a small tank that looked like one of ours. The top of the tank was open, and the tankist was standing up with his fist clenched in the Loyalist salute. Most of the fellows were resting up against the wall of a building while Wolff went over to talk to the tankist. As soon as Wolff approached, the tankist pulled the turret shut. Wolff shouted: 'Run for cover!'

"I was dumbfounded. I couldn't move. I froze against a wall. I just stood there and watched what was happening on the opposite side of the street. The machine gun in the tank opened up on the men leaning against the wall. They looked as though they had been lined up for a firing squad, and they were gunned down. About twenty comrades lay in the street, close together, practically all wounded. Some fell down pretending to be dead, hoping the tank would leave. The wounded were screaming in terrible agony."

Lou was breathing heavily; his eyes looked as though they would pop from their sockets. He talked louder and faster as though in a hurry to finish the terrible story.

"The tank stopped firing," he continued, "and then it began moving straight for the bodies in the street. Some men were able to get up and run away, but the tank rolled over the others, the dead, and the wounded who couldn't get away. I heard the crunching of their bones. I smelled their blood. Finally, the tank left."

Lou stopped. He was sobbing, but there were no tears.

"I can still hear the bones cracking, and I still smell the blood." He buried his face in his hands.

I tried to talk to him, to console him, but it was no use. He didn't say another word.

I never saw him again. He was killed the next day in our counterattack to capture a hill near Caspe.

By the next evening we knew that we had to take the hills around

Caspe, where the fascist forces were stationed. We now had eight Russian tanks, manned by Russians, and we were joined by Canadians and Englishmen.

Under cover of darkness, we attacked a section of the fascist line on the hills. Our tanks fired over our heads to give the impression of artillery support; we threw hand grenades (some men even threw rocks), and we shrieked like hyenas as we charged up the hill. The fascists were taken by surprise and fled; we captured about thirty men, and the hill was ours.

Not long after, we again received word that the fascists had broken through and that we were once again almost encircled. A Spanish officer told us to break up into small units and go through the woods and over the hills, but to stay off the roads. This officer then set up a machine gun on one side of the road and was joined by a young American who volunteered to help him. The American was nineteen-year-old Rudy Haber, who had arrived in Spain only six weeks earlier. We later learned that Haber and the Spaniard were killed, but they succeeded in holding off the fascists so that the rest of us could get a head start.

After hours of walking through the woods with a group of about ten, the group got smaller and smaller as the men dropped off to go in different directions. Finally only Harry Hakim and I were left. We continued in a general northeast direction until we came to a farm. We could see the farmer working near his house.

"Think we ought to approach him?" Hakim asked.

"Why not?" I answered.

The farmer seemed very apprehensive as we approached. He couldn't know who we were. We explained that we were Americans in the International Brigades. At once he became very friendly. He confided to us that he was going to flee the farm, because he knew he would be shot as soon as the fascists got there. For the first time in his life, he told us, he owned the land that he worked on; it had been given to him by the Loyalist government. Formerly the land had been owned by the Catholic Church. This peasant, his father before him, and his grandfather before him had worked the land for the Church. He expected that in a day or two, the land would be in fascist hands. If he stayed, he believed he would be shot for "stealing" the land from the Church.

He then gave each of us two raw eggs, which we immediately ate, and a large bag of potatoes. We shook hands with him, wished him well, and were off again.

"Where the hell are we going?" I asked Hakim.

"I don't know, but to be safe, let's go north and east, to keep away from the fascists. We may end up in France, but we can always get back to Spain."

That night, we looked for the North Star and headed in that general direction. By midnight we were exhausted. We saw a barn not far away and decided to spend the night there.

As we entered the barn, we realized we were intruding on a group of six soldiers, sitting around a fire they had made in a huge can. They looked at us very warily, and one of the soldiers casually picked up his rifle and pointed it in our direction. They didn't say a word, just kept looking at us. I decided I had better speak up, so I said, "Nosotros Internacionales, quince brigada."

Hearing that, they all smiled broadly and let us know that they too were Internationals, Germans from the Thaelmann Battalion. We shook hands all around and showed them the potatoes we had received from the Spanish farmer. They had some meat and were about to cook it. They said they would cook it with our potatoes and share the meal with us. We asked them to awaken us when the food was ready, and we went off to the side and fell asleep.

It was dawn when we awoke; we looked around for the Germans, but the barn was empty.

"The dirty bastards," I muttered. "Now we have nothing to eat. I'm starving."

Then we noticed a large can sitting on top of some red-hot ashes. In it were meat, potatoes, and vegetables, still warm, a wonderful stew. We gulped it down, feeling thankful that the German comrades had not forgotten us. After feasting, we continued our march through the wooded hills, keeping close to the road.

Just before evening, we saw some movement up the road. Coming into view was a group of soldiers. We knew they were ours, because they were all in torn and tattered uniforms. A bit farther on, we saw a group of about thirty men sitting on the side of the road.

We crept up closer to listen and heard them speaking in English. We decided to chance it and came out of the woods.

The first person I saw was Marty Sullivan. He threw his arms around me and shouted, "I was told that you'd been killed."

For the next few minutes I was surrounded by hand clasps, hugs, and the kind of greetings that only the dead who turn up alive can receive.

Once again, John Gates was in charge. We stayed put until the next day, by which time we had grown to over fifty men, about half of us Americans, Canadians, and British, the other half Spaniards.

And once again we were on the move, staying near, but off, the road. We moved slowly in the woods, going mostly north and east toward Batea. We continued to pick up stragglers, who, needless to say, were overjoyed at being with a larger group, organized and disciplined. We continued the march for about two more days, stopping once in a while for an hour or two. We had no food, and the hunger pangs became unbearable. All I could think of was food. Fortunately, we still had plenty of water.

Finally we joined a larger unit where Vladimir Copic, commander of the Fifteenth Brigade, was in charge. We were delighted to see more comrades alive and well.

Now we were a group of about two hundred men, including about seventy Americans. And once again we were told that we would have to put up a stand here, to try to end the fascist advance. Most of us grumbled and cursed, but despite the despair and the heartaches there was, strangely enough, a good deal of enthusiasm for the action. We were actually glad to be told that we could still put up a fight, that not everything was lost.

All during the retreats, Pat Reid had been ill. Ever since I had first met him, he had had a bad cough, but now I noticed that he was coughing up blood. I kept urging him to try to get to a hospital, but he always refused. He just wanted to be at the front with the men. Even when we were resting in the rear, he refused to see a doctor.

At about this time during the retreats, Dave Doran told me he was sending Reid to the rear.

"That's great," I said. "That guy is really sick, always coughing up blood. He needs attention."

"No, that's not why I'm sending him to the rear," said Doran. "He's doing a lot of harm, always talking against the Communist Party."

I was shocked. I knew Pat's heart would break if he were sent to the rear for that reason.

"But Dave, he's talked against the party for a year now, ever since he's been with the Lincolns. He's probably the best soldier in the battalion. Even Steve Nelson admired him. They always argued, yet Steve knew he was a good soldier and a good anti-fascist. He hasn't changed the position of a single communist soldier."

A little later, Pat came to me, looking like he was in real misery. "I'm being kicked out of the battalion," he said, crestfallen. "The head commie told me that I'm a bad boy, doing the fascists' job, by knocking the party." I told Pat that Doran knew he was sick, always heard him coughing, and probably wanted him to get medical care in the rear. But this was at a time when everybody in the rear was returning to the front, even many wounded soldiers. Pat knew better and he wouldn't buy my story.[4]

A few days after Pat had left the battalion, Dave Doran was killed. He and Merriman had walked into a fascist camping ground. We heard that they were both captured and shot on the spot.

On the last day of March we were told, once again, that we were surrounded. We would have to fight our way to Gandesa. This time, I took off with Sullivan, again walking through the woods, staying near the road but out of sight, going mainly east. And, of course, there was no food.

We arrived at Batea the next afternoon. The town was quiet, with a few families beginning to move east toward the Ebro. We saw a lot of activity around an old building that looked like a barn. Actually, it was a warehouse, where tons and tons of food had been stored for the soldiers at the front.

An American in charge of the warehouse told us: "Take as much as you can carry and let the civilians fill up their carts. The fascists are expected to be here any day, or even any hour. We don't want to burn the food, so we are giving it to the peasants."

Sully and I took some cans of condensed milk, canned meat, and fruit. Much of the rice, beans, and flour was in fifty- and one-hundred-pound sacks and impossible for us to carry. We helped dozens of peasants load their carts with the food and finally left in search of our headquarters.

Refugees were already crowding the road, many with carts and wagons full of the food from the warehouse. They were heading toward the Ebro River. We were walking not to the east now, but in the opposite direction, toward the west, where the fighting was taking place. The noise of the battle had abated; we walked slowly, hardly talking. We felt uneasy about going toward the front when we had been in retreat for three weeks. A few miles down the road we stopped some men from the British battalion who were walking rapidly toward the rear.

"What happened at the front today?" I asked.

"What happened! What didn't happen! Nearly our entire battalion was captured or killed, and we're getting the hell out of here," one of them shouted at us. Then they all began talking at once. That morning the battalion had been ordered to make contact with the fascists. There was no front line, the fascists having smashed it the day before. Somehow the British had found themselves in a little opening between some trees and sat down to rest. Tanks emerged from behind the trees, surrounding them. The British had been told that our tanks were just ahead of them, so they thought these were friendly tanks. Their commander approached one of the tanks to get some information. After talking for half a minute, the men were startled to see the commander raise his hands over his head. Some of the men began to run to the rear. The tanks opened fire on them while the rest were surrounded and surrendered. Only a few men had gotten away.[5]

Sully and I reached Fifteenth Brigade headquarters that night, after being picked up by one of our transmissions trucks. We had walked about fifteen miles, making a wrong turn at one point and going north instead of west, walking more or less parallel with the fascist line. But we were glad to be with the brigade again, surrounded by our comrades.

At headquarters we were given food and told to get some rest in a barn. After a few hours of sleep, I was awakened by someone shouting my name. I had to report to our commander, who told me to get to the Lincoln Battalion telephone switchboard control. Harry Hakim walked there with me. He told me that the battalion was stationed about half a mile ahead of the switchboard, and that nothing devastating had happened to the Americans the day before, although the British had been almost wiped out. We arrived at our destination just before dawn, and Hakim returned to headquarters.

The sun was just coming up; it was cold, and I wrapped my blanket tightly around me. I stared at the switchboard, expecting the telephone to buzz. Normie Berkowitz was there, sleeping on his back, snoring evenly and softly, more a groan than a snore. His moaning-snoring gave me the jitters, but I didn't have the heart to awaken him. I knew he must have been exhausted.

There was a tremendous boulder near us, about a foot thick and perfectly flat. I thought that if a hole were dug under it, it would act as a good roof for about five of us in case of a shelling or bombing attack. The greater part of the boulder was embedded in the earth, which rose sharply behind us, so that there was no danger of the rock falling on us. I decided to begin digging right away. The earth was hard, so the digging was slow. And it awakened Normie.

"Hi, Harry!" Normie was always so damn good-natured that even seconds after waking in this hellhole he was cheerful.

"Hi, Norm! What's going on?" I responded, trying to be equally cheerful.

"What the hell do I know." He grinned and continued: "There's fighting going on all over the place. There's a road about five miles to our east where the fascists are banging away with everything they have—planes, tanks, artillery, and troops. If they break through over there we're cooked, because it will mean that those bastards will have surrounded us, and we'll be cut off. They don't give a damn what we do here, how far we advance, because they figure that the farther we advance, the deeper we get into their trap. We captured two of their men yesterday, and a truck too. But that's only chicken feed compared to what they're doing. You watch, within half an hour you'll see their planes playing games out there. Nothing will happen here. But everything depends on our east."

We spent the rest of the morning digging and watching the fascist planes bombing exactly where Normie said they would.

The phone rang. It was John "Wisconsin" Cookson, who had taken the place of Pat Reid as commander of the transmissions group. His words were sharp, clear, and brief.

"Let Wolff know you're moving. Take the switchboard and all the wire and phones that you have. Pick up whatever lines you can between you and Brigade headquarters. Report here as soon as possible, within an hour at most."

"What's happened?" I asked.

"Nothing. Just do as you're told."

But I knew what had happened. The bombing and shelling had kept up all day in the east. It was obvious that our lines were breaking and the men were retreating. The battle was moving slowly to the rear.

Joe Byrnes was running up the hill past us, looking worried. He obviously had instructions for the battalion.

Normie and I cursed lustily and loudly while rolling up the wire. What the goddamn hell was so important about a little wire during such a quick retreat? Nevertheless, we rolled up as much as we could carry. Sully and a comrade we called Frenchy were coming toward us, also picking up wire. "Looks bad," was all we could get from them.

When we got to Brigade headquarters, we sat on the side of the road awaiting orders. One of our tanks came from the rear, not the front. Paul Goldberg talked with the tankist and then ran over to us shouting excitedly that he had been told that the crossroad had been captured by the fascists, that our way was blocked, and that the front was now in front of us, behind us, all around us. Joe Byrnes rushed toward Goldberg and shouted, "You son of a bitch, what are you trying to do—start a panic here with your rumors? Keep your lousy mouth shut."

About five minutes later, Copic's car came speeding back and screeched to a halt. Copic stepped out of the car, wiping the sweat off his forehead. Now there was no doubt as to who had control of the crossroad. We looked at Copic, awaiting his orders. He raised his hand and waved it in an easterly direction. The wordless order was clear enough. We were surrounded, and again we would have to go through the woods to get through the fascist lines.

We began our march, and it was one o'clock in the morning before we could sit down for a rest. Although there had been about fifty men when we started, there were now only eleven—all transmissions men. The other forty or so had thought it best to break up into small groups.

All evening Sully and I had been trying to shake off Cookson, because in the past he had always seemed to be somewhat hysterical. But we couldn't get rid of him, and now, to our surprise, Cookson was in charge. He seemed to be the only one who knew what to do and was as calm as a Boy Scout leader.

Rumors were going around that Cookson had broken down at one of the battles and had been sent to the rear to recuperate. After a while, when he was well again, he had asked to do the most dangerous jobs possible in Spain. He was sent to work with Internationals and Spaniards behind fascist lines. He was an expert at making bombs; many times he also went out on dangerous missions and won high praise for his daring feats.

Before coming to Spain, Cookson had been an instructor of mathematics at the University of Wisconsin. His reputation was unblemished, and he was considered to be brilliant.[6] However, here in Spain, he had great difficulty getting along with the men. I remember one time, shortly after he was given command of the transmissions group, I was sitting with Jerry Cook, Jack Shafran, Normie Berkowitz, and Marty Sullivan. Cookson ordered one of us to do something. Jack Shafran looked at him and said, "Fuck you." Cookson was so startled that he just stood there staring at us. Suddenly, sounding like a spoiled child, he began to scream, almost screeching, "Fuck you, fuck you." We watched him in silence, and then we all began to laugh. Cookson stood there dumbfounded, surprised at our reaction, until a big grin spread over his face.

"That's the first time in my life I ever used that word," he explained. He was rather proud of himself.

So here we were, some weeks later, eleven retreaters in the woods, with Cookson in charge. We stopped to take inventory. Everyone was carrying a phone or a spool of wire, or some other transmission equipment on his back. And only one man had a rifle.

Cookson said: "From now on we walk single file, without talking. We are going either north or east until we get through the fascist lines. We'll keep going all night, and then at dawn we'll decide what to do next."

We began our march. The night was dark, and the stars seemed particularly brilliant. I wanted to walk faster, but I was too tired. I had had only a few hours' sleep the night before and none at all the night before that. My blanket didn't keep me warm; my hands were bleeding and aching from digging trenches the day before. My feet were sore from walking over stones with holes in my shoes. Under my breath I cursed the grapevines that kept scratching at my feet.

It was the beginning of April. My thoughts wandered to home, to New York, to my mother, and to my brother Ben, in their tiny but comfortable apartment. What the hell am I doing here, in the middle of the night, cold, tired, hungry, scared, walking in the woods, my head bent, watching the feet in front of me? Would I be alive tomorrow? Would I ever again sleep in a warm bed?

We stopped to rest. About a mile ahead of us, tracer bullets sailed gracefully through the air. The bullets seemed to be going in all directions. We could clearly hear the crack of rifles; the fighting was not far off. Cookson went to see what was going on while we rested. My admiration for Cookson was growing by leaps and bounds. He had had as little sleep as any of us, or less, yet here he was, calm, collected, seemingly tireless, and going out on the most dangerous ventures.

Sully shook me. I had fallen asleep.

"Come on, we're moving."

Oh Christ, if only we could rest just a little more—just ten minutes more to sleep. What's the use of just walking, hour after hour?

Sully was determined to get me up. Finally, I dragged myself to my feet and began to move. My eyes were riveted on the feet in front of me. I concentrated on those feet—to whom did they belong? It suddenly was of the greatest importance, but I couldn't lift my head to see who was attached to those feet. Ah yes, of course, I recognized those tattered shoes—Normie was on top of those feet! Good ol' Norm, still with us!

I closed my eyes and tried to sleep while walking.

Impossible! Those damned grapevine bushes kept pricking my feet. Now I was wide awake.

"Everyone sit down and keep quiet," Cookson whispered. We heard footsteps coming our way. We didn't move; we hardly breathed. Soon a line of soldiers marching in single file passed about ten feet from us. Each soldier carried a rifle. They glanced at us as they passed. No one said a word. We just sat, and they walked past us. A few minutes later, when they were some distance from us, Normie said, "Who the hell could they be?" None of us knew.

"They were as scared as we were," Cookson remarked.

We continued to rest against a stone wall, all of us shaking from the cold night air. Cookson was pacing back and forth. He looked at his watch and let us know that it was just three o'clock; we had three more hours before dawn.

Just as we were about to resume our march, we heard something that sounded similar to carts being pulled on the road. The sound drew nearer.

"Sounds like peasants moving with their carts. Good idea to follow them. They know their way around here better than anyone," whispered Cookson.

We all thought it a fine idea and moved closer to the road. In a few minutes we were facing not peasants, but soldiers, marching in columns of three. Burros were pulling small artillery pieces.

I glanced at Cookson, who had already turned his beret inside out to hide his officer's stripes. He quickly whispered to us to stay quiet and to say nothing. If any questions were asked, he would simply say, "transmisiones."

There was no doubt that they were fascists. The soldiers were in high spirits, maintained good order, had clean uniforms, and marched in formation; their officers rode on horses.

A mounted officer stopped near us and looked us over, obviously trying to figure out who we were. The last of the column was just then going past us, so we got onto the road and joined the march at the end of their line.

The officer seemed satisfied and galloped ahead. So here we were, bringing up the rear of the advancing fascists, who were, in effect, routing us.

I kept studying the sides of the road, looking for a good place to run, should it become necessary. The telephone strap was cutting into my shoulder, lice made me itch, and I was cold and hungry—but none of it mattered. Now we just had to stay alive. The fear inside me was painful. Would the officers come back and place us under arrest? Would they shoot us on the spot? Would they torture us? Was this the way I would die?

Could I really be marching with fascist troops?!

I looked at Sullivan, who was marching next to me. He looked at me and whispered, "God, but I'm hungry. I wish these bastards would stop and dish out some food."

We were going around a sharp curve in the road, still bringing up the fascist rear, when we heard horses coming back toward us. Cookson stopped, extended his hands to stop us, and motioned for us to sit down on the side of the road against the hill that rose sharply on our right. Quickly we sat. The officers reached the end of their line and stopped, evidently reluctant to leave their men and search for us, afraid of being ambushed.

We listened as they held a conference, speaking in very subdued voices. The only word we could make out was "rojos" (reds). After about a minute, they galloped back to their men. We immediately raced across the road and vanished into the woods.

About three hours later we found ourselves on top of a high hill, able to look over a good part of the country. The sun was just coming up. Sully and I could think of nothing but rest and sleep. We turned to Cookson and suggested that we spend the day sleeping in some safe place, with everyone getting a turn at keeping lookout. Then with nightfall we would continue our march.

Cookson wouldn't hear of it.

"First of all," he argued, "what are you going to do about food? We'll starve if we spend the day here. Second, and more important, it's dangerous here. Those fascists we marched with last night are going to set up a line as soon as they make contact with our troops."

"But it would be easier for them to spot us in the daytime," said Sully. "We'd have a better chance of getting through at night."

Cookson ended the discussion with an argument we couldn't answer. "By night they'll have an effective line at the front. Then just try to get through! All we have is a single rifle."

And so we marched on, staying high in the hills. After about an hour, we saw a highway below us, with a few soldiers on it.

"They look like our men," said Cookson.

We scurried down the hill just as some shots rang out. No bullets whistled over our heads, but soon it sounded like a battle was taking place somewhere behind us. We got to the road and with much relief saw that indeed these were our men. We asked an officer for instructions. He advised us to head east for the Ebro River where new lines were being formed.

We had about fifteen miles to go, but at least we would get some sleep and, we hoped, something to eat.

After a while, we reached the town of Gandesa. The civilian population was frantically loading carts with belongings and food, in anticipation of a fascist aerial attack. The scene was very similar to what we had seen in Batea a few days earlier. People were piling sacks of sugar, rice, bread, coffee, canned goods, and tobacco onto their carts. One old woman was trying desperately to drag a tremendous sack of sugar along the road, but she could hardly budge it. Small children, five and six years old, were running like mad with their hands full of food. Women were screaming at the children to hurry and get more, while they guarded the carts as though they were gold mines, which, in a manner of speaking, they were. Everyone kept looking up at the skies with terror in their eyes, always expecting the fascist planes to begin an attack.

Sully and I went into the warehouse, which consisted of one very large room that looked more like a gymnasium. An officer was urging all the people to take as much as they could, to leave nothing, or as little as possible, for the fascists.

Sully and I helped some of the women load their carts, and we, along with other soldiers, filled our knapsacks with some canned food, tobacco, and bread.

The road was now crowded with soldiers and civilians going in the same direction. There were no group formations, there was no discipline. Officers were not giving orders; everyone just moved ahead toward the Ebro. Many women were carrying babies. Some had carts loaded with pots and pans and food from the warehouses. Tired, thin burros hauled wagons laden with mattresses and chairs. The only civilian men were elderly. The soldiers were tired, dirty, and hungry. Hardly anyone spoke. Although Sully and I wanted desperately to rest a bit, we knew we couldn't risk it. The enemy was too close; we had to push on.

Our march continued. Hour after hour we trudged along in silence. We were perhaps seven miles out of Gandesa when suddenly and without warning fascist fighter planes appeared overhead. They were terrifyingly low, no more than 150 feet above ground level. There was no time to get off the road, so everyone just dropped where they were as the planes' machine guns opened fire. The attack lasted no more than two minutes; the planes vanished as quickly as they had appeared.

Now, all hell broke loose. The scene was one of utter chaos. The silence of our march was shattered by the screams of the wounded and of survivors desperately looking for their loved ones. There were many casualties, almost all civilians.

Sully and I began loading the wounded and dead on wagons. An American truck approached us, heading toward Gandesa. We told the driver to turn around, that it was too late, that the fascists were already there. The truck driver agreed to take as many people as he could to the hospital, so the three of us began loading the truck with the wounded.

One young woman, disoriented and bloodied, stood nearby. I was helping her board the truck when suddenly she began yelling for her baby. Sully and I looked around to see if we could find the child, but someone whispered to us, "Muerto, muerto." The baby was lying on the road lifeless. Sully approached the woman and tried to explain that her baby was dead. But she still called out for it. I watched Sully carry the little bundle to the truck and put the baby in the mother's lap. The mother cuddled the baby as if it were still alive.

The grisly task of loading the wounded and dead onto wagons continued. We worked in silence. I can still see Sully's face distorted with anger. We never talked about this incident again.

Our journey continued. Sully and I were covered with blood, but not our own. The march seemed endless, but several hours later we reached the Ebro.

The riverfront was buzzing with excitement. There were about two hundred men here, including about twenty-five Americans. Everyone was busy digging trenches, distributing rifles, and talking with confidence and spirit. The newspaper *Frente Rojo,* in everyone's hands, had a banner headline: "NO PASARÁN." The slogan seemed to be on the minds and in the hearts of every soldier there.

Brigade commander Copic stood in the middle of the road with his arms folded across his chest, giving orders. A young Spaniard came running to Copic, reporting that the fascists were approaching. Copic told the Spanish officers to prepare the men for action.

I looked to see if there were any familiar faces and saw Benny Kasinap, a comrade from Baltimore, sitting on the side of the road, surrounded by a dozen or so hand grenades.

"I never played with these things," he said. "I'll see if I know how to use them. Suppose I climb up this tree and drop them down on the fascists as they come by."

Someone quickly explained to Benny that he would be the first casualty, because grenades explode upward. Benny abandoned the idea. Benny had a very queer sense of humor; he often told strange stories about himself just to shock people. Instead of taking his stories with a grain of salt, many comrades took him seriously; they were, indeed, shocked, and avoided him as much as possible. I knew him to be a courageous, warm, and funny fellow, who many times placed himself in jeopardy to help wounded comrades.[7]

Suddenly Cookson came into view. He instructed Sully and me to report to transmissions headquarters on the other side of the river. This was one order that we were only too glad to carry out. A guard stopped us at the bridge, but the telephone equipment and the magic word "transmisiones" got us through.

A transmissions truck picked us up on the other side of the bridge, in Mora de Nueve, and we were on our way to headquarters. We could have made better time walking, for the road was filled with refugees, cars, and trucks, but at least we were off our feet. One car went past us heading toward the bridge and the front. I recognized Ernest Hemingway, Herbert Matthews of the *New York Times,* Joe North of the *Daily Worker,* and Louis Fischer, a well-known liberal writer. One of the men on our truck yelled to the writers that it was dangerous to go in that direction, that the fascists would be setting up a line there at any moment, and that the front was shaky and fluid. The four correspondents just smiled at us and continued. But not for long. About ten minutes later, the same car passed us, now heading away from the bridge.

When we finally arrived at transmissions headquarters, Sully and I made a dash for the kitchen. To our great delight, there were Normie Berkowitz, Jerry Cook, and Jack Shafran, my trade union comrades, still alive and well.

"We thought you were dead or captured," we cried out. We hugged and laughed and cried a little too. Then I filled my platter with a delicious stew. I finished half a loaf of bread and three plates of food with two or three cups of wine. I remember that meal to this day.

After a while, I wandered over to a secluded spot, and just as I was getting comfortably settled to take a long overdue nap, a loud explosion came from the rear.

"That's the bridge. We just blew it up," I heard someone say, before I fell into a deep, twelve-hour sleep.

For the first time in a month, I felt a sense of relief. The Ebro River was wide and fast flowing; the fascists were on the west side of it, and we were on the east. Now the job was to get all the men together, to reorganize, retrain, and get ready for the next action, whenever and wherever that would be.

There were only about fifty Americans, some Canadians, and twenty or thirty Spaniards, hardly enough even for a small company. But every day for the next few days, one, two, or three Americans would show up. Some of the new arrivals included John Gates, Milton Wolff, Joe Brandt,

George Watt, and Yale Stuart. Each new arrival was greeted with shouts of joy and expressions of amazement. The nights were filled with stories of how each of us had gotten through the fascist lines; quite a few had had to swim the Ebro River. We learned of the capture of many Americans, including Hy Wallach, Sid Rosenblatt, Leon Tenor, Bob Steck, and Charles Keith.

One day in early April I was delighted—and also saddened—to find John Murra with the battalion. His fluency in most of the languages spoken by members of the International Brigades had made him practically indispensable at various headquarters, but when we had worked together in Albacete he had told me how much he wanted to be at the front, despite his usefulness at the rear. He had heard in Barcelona that the Lincolns had been decimated and had made up his mind to join what was left of the battalion. One day he just left his office post and, all alone, started heading south. For days he wandered through the Spanish countryside searching for the battalion, until one day he was stopped by Spanish military police and arrested because he didn't have proper papers. He was imprisoned at a work farm for, of all things, having "deserted" from the rear to find his way to the front! He did manage to persuade the authorities that his intentions were only to help the Loyalist effort, and because things were going badly at the front, they agreed to let him join the Lincolns. And now here he was, seeming to me much happier than when he had been in an office in Albacete. The fellows in his company took a real liking to him, and he became very popular with all the Americans.

After a few days we moved to a position about two miles behind the Ebro. Our ranks were now replenished by new, young Spaniards and also some Americans, including my friends Joe Rehil, Bill Wheeler, and Joe Gordon, all of whom were in Spain for the second time, having been wounded earlier and sent home for treatment. Impossible as it had seemed a few weeks earlier, the battalion was again at full strength.

We trained for some time but saw no action. I wrote home a lot during this period. In one letter, I mentioned a restaurant I remember quite well:

July 8, 1938
Dear Sal and Hy:

I just mailed a short post card to you a little while ago and
then received your letter with the cigarettes. I also received a letter from Vivienne with cigarettes. The boys haven't had any cigarettes for weeks and have been smoking dried leaves. I gave all
the cigarettes to the heavy smokers, since they almost go crazy
without cigarettes and I don't miss them so much as they do.
There is a bad shortage of tobacco for some reason or other, so
that the ones you send will come in very handy. Gosh, you have
no idea how badly I feel when I realize how much you want me
to come home. I think I explained the situation before. There is
no repatriation except for the wounded. I'm sure that I'll be
home in 1938 and I don't think it will be so long from now. How
happy I'll be when I see you all again. I imagine I'll hug you all to
death. I've imagined myself coming into your house so many
times and trying to be nonchalant—but still I dream about it.

I've just returned from two days in Barcelona. I ate my meals
in a Jewish place. The meals were delicious—just like mom's.
Even shtrudel and blintzes and chicken soup and chicken and all
that stuffing. I heard Jewish spoken again. Was I homesick. And
now I miss mom more than ever.

Love,
Harry[8]

I remember many stories from this period, sometimes mere snippets of
stories. I remember one night when we were told to get ready to move
again, this time farther back to the rear. The weather was dreadful. It
rained and rained, and soon we were all soaked to the skin. We walked
for hours, wet, cold, sleepy, cranky, demoralized. Finally, a little after
midnight, we were told to bed down in an area that was flooded and
muddy. It was still raining. I took off my soggy knapsack, put it in a pud-
dle about six inches deep, put my two folded wet blankets against a big
tree trunk, with my rear end and feet in at least six inches of water. I
cursed and bitched and thought of my warm bed at home, covered with

dry, clean sheets. I closed my eyes but couldn't fall asleep. I remembered Yale Stuart's stories about Camp Unity, where he had been a lifeguard. Thinking about his stories made me chuckle, and I soon fell fast asleep.

I awoke at dawn; the rain had stopped and the sky was clearing. I gazed around me to get my bearings and then noticed a small hut on a hill, only about fifteen yards away. I walked over to the cabin and found that it had one room with a fireplace; it was dry and, surprisingly, empty. The hut became headquarters for the Lincolns and was immediately dubbed "Tammany Hall."

We began our training again, leaving camp for maneuvers for a good part of each day. The days were long, hot, and dry. The food was terrible, just like everything else around us. The men were angry, restless, and quarrelsome. One day, as the headquarters staff lined up at noon for the usual lousy chow, a soldier wormed his way into the line, just ahead of me.

"Get your ass out of here," I bellowed. "Get to the rear of the line."

"Go fuck yourself," he answered.

I was mad as all hell. I grabbed him by the shoulder, pulled him out of the line, and said, "Put up your fists, you lousy bastard." I was aching for a fight, and he was smaller than I.

He looked at me with scared eyes and shuffled off to the end of the line. Man, I felt tough. I sure showed that son of a bitch.

The next day at lunch time, the same thing happened. Only this time it was Tom O'Flaherty, who was a few inches taller and about forty pounds heavier than I.

Again I yelled: "O'Flaherty, get your ass to the end of the line, or I'll knock the shit out of you."

What the hell, it had worked the day before. But that goddamned O'Flaherty didn't scare as easily. He looked at me, smiled, and said, "I'm staying here. What are you going to do about it?"

I stared at him, still itching for a fight, but not quite as anxiously.

"Aren't you going to pull me out of the line and knock the shit out of me?" he grinned.

I kept staring at him, conscious of the fact that everyone was now watching us. I had been such a hero yesterday, but I wasn't so sure now.

"You were ready to fight yesterday, Fisher. Are you still ready?"

With all those eyes on me, the big hero of yesterday, I had to say something.

"OK, step out and put up your dukes," I answered not very enthusiastically.

"Let's go into the woods and settle this," O'Flaherty said quietly. Normie Berkowitz came along as the second for O'Flaherty, and Marty Sullivan was my second.

While walking to the woods I said to myself, "What the hell have I gotten into now?" I wasn't so angry anymore, but I sure was scared. What the hell, I reasoned. It can't be as bad as getting a bullet shot through me.

Finally, it was time to fight. O'Flaherty started dancing around me. His left fist kept jabbing me in my nose, eyes, and mouth. I fell down a few times, even though his jabs were really light. I swung roundhouses at him but missed by a mile; I couldn't even get close to his face. This went on for about four minutes; I was exhausted, but O'Flaherty seemed as fresh as when we started. I began to hope that he would hit me hard enough so that I would be knocked out, or maybe I could fake it.

I was mightily relieved when O'Flaherty stopped and stuck his hand out to me. I grabbed it eagerly. We shook, and I said, "So you've had enough! Let this be a lesson to you." O'Flaherty burst out laughing and put his arm around my shoulder. We returned to the chow line. Everyone stared at my face. My nose was bleeding, my eyes swollen, my lips cut, but I felt better.

"What happened to you, Fisher?"

"Oh, I taught this son of a bitch a lesson. I knocked the shit out of him. Look, I got him to go to the end of the line."

O'Flaherty grinned and said, "Yeah, I'm not gonna tangle with this tough guy anymore."

Later that day, John Murra got a look at me and asked what had happened. I told him about the fight with O'Flaherty. John was outraged.

"Didn't you know that he was a collegiate welterweight champion?"

No, I had not known that. But I assured John that O'Flaherty never really hurt me, that he just toyed with me. If he had wanted to, he could have put me to sleep permanently.[9]

O'Flaherty and I became good friends. Subsequently we learned that we had a mutual friend, Hank Forbes, who was district organizer for the Communist Party in New York.

A few months later O'Flaherty was killed in action. The news left me dejected and miserable.

The day after my fight with O'Flaherty, Jack Shafran, together with other men of Company Three, lined up for water. Dried fish had been a staple food for some time now, and the men were anxious to fill their canteens.

Jack, near the end of the line, watched Captain Tony DeMaio, newly arrived from his rear position in Barcelona, push his way to the front of the line. His shiny boots and clean uniform were a sharp contrast to the torn clothes and shoes worn by the men on the line.

Jack, imbued with the spirit of equal rights for all, and especially for soldiers on the water line, shouted, "Hey, you bastard, get your fucking ass to the end of the line."

DeMaio was furious. He marched down the line and demanded to know who had said that.

Jack, unintimidated, answered, "I did. Who the fucking hell do you think you are?"

"Can't you see that I am a captain?"

"I don't give a shit if you're a general. Get to the end of the line, or go fuck yourself."

DeMaio drew his pistol and barked, "You're under arrest for insubordination."

After asking Jack for directions to the battalion headquarters, off they marched to see the battalion commander, Milt Wolff, who listened to the story, furrowed his brow, and advised DeMaio, "This is not my problem. Take it up with the company commander."

The commander, a Spanish captain, spoke very little English. John Murra was called in to act as translator.

The captain listened intently to Murra's translation of the incident. Puzzled, he turned to Murra and asked him to explain this word "fucking." Murra explained that the word could be used as an adjective or a verb.

For a moment the captain was silent; then he sighed deeply, and spoke haltingly in broken English. "You Americans are very strange. From your actions and comments, sometimes fucking is good, other times fucking is bad. From now on there is to be no more fucking in this company. As for the punishment for insubordination, go dig a latrine."

Jack's two best friends, Jerry Cook and Normie Berkowitz, enjoyed this incident enormously. And, in keeping with the spirit of the moment, Jerry and Normie volunteered to be Jack's guards while Jack worked on an old latrine, extending it by about ten feet and making it about five feet deeper. Jack began digging with a shovel, while Jerry and Normie urged him on, pointing empty rifles at him. At one point, Jerry tried to tighten his wristwatch, when it slipped from his fingers and fell into the used latrine, into all the stinking filth.

The digging stopped, and the three friends somberly discussed how they could retrieve the watch. Finally, Jack came up with a solution.

"Jerry, I'll hold one of your legs and Normie will hold the other. We'll lower you till you grab the watch, and then we'll bring you up." Jerry agreed. So the two held Jerry by his legs and lowered him until he picked up his watch.

"OK, fellas, I've got it. Lift me up. It stinks like hell down here. Get me out of this mess."

"Hey Jerry, not so fast," yelled Jack. "We'll lift you up only if you promise to finish the latrine."

"The hell I will. You're the guy who's being punished. Come on, I can't stand it down here any more. Get me up!"

"Jerry, you better promise to dig this latrine, or we may drop you. You better agree."

Jerry finally agreed, and his two friends pulled him up. Jack handed Jerry the shovel and said, "start digging."

Not unexpectedly, all three of them ended up taking turns digging and finished the job in a few days.

During this period, rumors that the Internationals were going home became rampant. The most popular song among the feisty Americans went as follows:

I want to go home
I want to go home
Machine guns they rattle
And cannons they roar
I don't wanna go to the front anymore
Take me over the sea
Where the fascists can't get at me
Oh my, I'm too young to die
I want to go home.

One day John Gates, Brigade commissar, called all the Americans in the battalion to a meeting. Gates was short, ramrod straight, humorless, tough, and aloof. Most of his time was spent at Brigade headquarters with the officers; he had very little contact with the men. Gates was noted for his courage, but few knew him to be warm or friendly.

The Americans, in a sullen mood, all gathered near "Tammany Hall." As soon as Gates arrived, he climbed on a nearby stone wall and faced over 150 men. His face was grim, hard, almost cruel. He had heard the rumors about the Internationals going home. His response was that the rumors were started by right-deviationists, left-deviationists, Trotsky-ites, and other troublemakers in our ranks. He firmly announced that none of us would be going home until the war was over.

"You all volunteered to fight to the end, and only death or a bad wound will end it for you."

The speech lasted about fifteen minutes. Gates glared at us, and we glared right back at him. Then he jumped off the stone wall and left immediately. We were amazed at his stupidity and even more demoralized by his lack of understanding. I heard someone say, "that son of a bitch."

The Lincoln Battalion had its share of weird characters, and one of them was Morris Mickenberg, a great storyteller and by far the best rumormonger in the battalion. The morning after the now-infamous speech by Gates, Mickenberg sat down with a few of us, including Cook, Shafran, Sullivan, Berkowitz, Rehil, and me.

"Wow, did I have a dream last night. A plan had been arranged for all the Americans to be sent home in a hurry. We were to be flown to New

York in a squadron of large planes; we were to parachute out over Central Park, where a huge demonstration welcoming us home was to take place.

"There we were, all of us already seated in the planes, waiting for the takeoff, when all of a sudden all the motors stopped, and we were told to get off. The planes could not leave. When we got off the planes, we saw what it was that had stopped us. The airplanes were surrounded by gates; there were gates, gates all around the planes."

Needless to say, there was no love lost between Gates and Mickenberg.

After the retreats, Jim Lardner, of the well-known literary family, joined the Lincoln Battalion. I remember the day Lardner came on board. Sully and I were at the switchboard in battalion headquarters; Commander Milt Wolff was in the headquarters when Lardner was brought in.

"Look here, Lardner," he said gruffly. "You're going to be treated just like any other soldier in this outfit. We don't play favorites."

Lardner looked at Wolff and said quietly, "I don't expect to be treated any differently than the rest of the soldiers."

Lardner went off to join Company Three, which included Murra, Shafran, Berkowitz, and Cook. Lardner was a slight, pleasant-looking fellow, very unsoldierlike. He was polite and kind to everyone. Too good. When food was being served and everyone rushed to be first in line, Jim would always get to the end of the line and let anyone who wanted to push ahead of him. His English was precise and correct; he never cursed. Probably for these reasons, the men found it difficult to get along with him.

Now John Murra, also an intellectual, got along beautifully with the men; he was well liked from the beginning. One day, Jim asked John why he, Jim, couldn't reach the others, why he couldn't communicate with them. John was blunt with him.

"Because you're not one of the boys. You don't speak their language. And this business of always getting at the end of the chow line . . . stop being such a good guy."

Lardner changed; he became "one of the boys." He ran to be at the beginning of the line, sometimes he even tried to push ahead of some of the fellows. He also learned how to curse, and his four-letter words peppered every sentence. He wrote some wonderfully hilarious poems for the bulletin board, with a four-letter word on every line. He became tremendously popular.[10]

For a while, I shared a dugout with Yale Stuart and Ed Rolfe (a well-known progressive poet and newspaperman). One day Yale received a tremendous parcel from the Food Workers Union, to which he belonged. Ed and I licked our chops, thinking what our share of the package would be. With much fanfare and many loud exclamations, Yale opened his package and handed Ed and me two cigarettes and two bars of Hershey's chocolate. We were aghast.

But Yale was a very courageous soldier. Later on, during our offensive across the Ebro, Yale was wounded and lost an arm.

During this three-month training period, there was plenty of time for bull sessions, and some pretty good stories were told.

Tommy Lloyd, a good-looking, blond Irishman, told a story that gave us all a good laugh. During one recent battle, one of our food trucks had come under fascist fire. The driver jumped out of the truck, ran to our lines, and left the truck between us and the fascists. Tommy noticed two fascists near the truck, obviously trying to get the food for their men. Tommy rushed over to Wolff and said, "Lend me your pistol. I'll return it to you later." Wolff started to say something, but Tommy grabbed the pistol and crawled out to the truck, which was about fifty yards away. He got behind the fascists, one of whom was an officer, and yelled, "¡Manos arriba!" The two startled fascists put their hands up, and Tommy, with his pistol pointed at their backs, marched them to our side. He turned the prisoners and the pistol over to Wolff, who had tensely watched the entire action.

"Tommy," said Wolff, "I tried to tell you that this pistol . . . it doesn't work. It's broken."

Tommy, in telling the story, claimed he almost had a heart attack.

Alvah Bessie was another interesting comrade. His best friend was Aaron Lopoff. It was seldom that Bessie would be seen without Lopoff at his side. Whenever there was a lull during the retreats, a large group of men would gather around these two to listen to and frequently participate in their discussions on literature, history, economics, theater, and the arts. The discussions would go on for hours, sometimes evoking heated arguments. They were interesting and stimulating; I always looked forward to the next session.

Of all the events I recall from this period, one has had a particularly powerful effect on me all my life. It concerns an incident I've tried my best to forget, but can't. There were only two people I ever discussed it with in over fifty years—my wife, Ruth, and my friend John Murra. And I don't think we discussed it more than three or four times during all those many years.

It was the end of April 1938. I was called into battalion headquarters one day, where a certain lieutenant greeted me. "Harry," he said, "we have a job for you to do tonight." And then, rather simply: "There's a soldier who has deserted three times, and we want you to shoot him while he sleeps. The whole thing will take only a few minutes."

I was stunned. I couldn't believe what I was hearing. "What's his name?" I heard myself asking.

"Bernard Abramofsky."

I had heard the name before but had never met the man. Apparently, as the lieutenant went on to explain, Abramofsky had been with the Washington battalion until the Lincolns and Washingtons had become one battalion due to heavy casualties during the Brunete campaign. While the Washington battalion had been in training, Abramofsky and two of his friends had entertained soldiers and civilians with songs and skits. They were very popular.

Abramofsky's two friends were later killed in battle, I was told, and Abramofsky had become so full of fear that he simply could not function anymore. I was told that he had faked being wounded during the Brunete offensive, and that two soldiers had had to carry him a long way to an ambulance, while other seriously wounded soldiers could not be cared for. Then he had deserted from the hospital.

After being captured and arrested, he had been taken back to the battalion. He then had deserted two more times.

For some time I stared at the lieutenant, and finally said, "I didn't come to Spain to kill Americans. I can't do it. I won't."

"Well, what do you think we should do with this deserter?" he asked me disdainfully.

"I don't know. Maybe give him a job in the rear. But he shouldn't be killed just because he is fearful. He's really a wounded soldier—mentally wounded."

"He's going to be shot. If you don't do it, then someone with more guts than you will."

Now my shock turned to anger. "Why don't you tell the son of a bitch who's ordering this to do it himself? Or doesn't *he* have enough guts?" My guess was that it was the brigade commissar, John Gates, who had ordered the execution. I had been through many tough situations with Gates during the recent retreats and had always found him to be calm and courageous. I thought very highly of him as an officer and as a leader, and yet I had always disliked him. He seemed to have no understanding or feeling for the men.

I left battalion headquarters in disgust and anger, but mostly in sadness. I could not understand how anyone could sentence a volunteer to death simply because fear made him incapable of being a good soldier.[11]

About two hours later, John Murra approached me. His jaw was twitching, and I could see that he was very upset. He told me that he had been called into headquarters and asked to shoot Abramofsky. I can't remember much about the conversation we had at that moment, but he also had indignantly refused to do the job. Neither of us could believe that this was happening.

John and I stood for some time near a stone fence that separated two farms and watched an artillery duel going on some miles away. We talked for a long time, until it was dark, about somehow warning Abramofsky, but we had no idea who or where he was. We were miserable beyond words.

Sometime later we heard a shot, not too far from us. We both knew immediately what it meant. Soon after, John and I parted without a word.[12]

I never heard the men talk about Abramofsky's death. I have no idea if most of the men even knew about it.

11. The Ebro Offensive

ON THE MORNING OF JULY 23, Joe North, correspondent for the *Daily Worker*, greeted us with: "Have you heard? The battalion is moving to the Ebro."

In about an hour came the official word. We were going on the offensive. We quickly got our communications equipment onto trucks and started out in the direction of the Ebro. Morale was very high. The Internationals were now hardened veterans who had taken everything the enemy had thrown at us. We were ready to do battle.

Most of the Spaniards in our ranks, however, were young kids, about eighteen years old, who had been recruited during the last few months. Few of them had any experience with warfare. Some nights earlier, the northern sky had become flaming red as a result of the aurora borealis. The sky flickered and danced, a beautiful sight. But many of the young Spaniards in our outfit had become frightened at the sight and had started to run to the rear. They had never witnessed such a sight before; they thought it had something to do with the war. It took a lot of explaining and patience to calm them.

In a few hours, the trucks dropped us off about a mile from the Ebro. We camped there for two days, listening to pep talks and military explanations of the offensive that would soon begin. Our aim was to capture the town of Gandesa, which was located on a strategic crossroad. If we captured this town, it would prevent the fascists from cutting the Loyalist territory in half and from reaching the Mediterranean.

In a way, we were all excited and exhilarated—the boredom was over. But all the old fears went through my mind once again. Would I live through this next action? Would I be crippled? How many more of my friends would be killed? With an effort, I brushed these thoughts away.

At about three o'clock in the morning, with the stars still shining brightly, we lined up and began heading for the Ebro River. "No smoking, no talking, no noise at all," we were warned. Ammunition had been distributed the evening before, and I had stuffed two hand grenades into my pocket. While walking quietly toward the river, I reached into my pocket and wrapped my fingers around one of the grenades. Something was wrong. The pin was gone. I thought perhaps I had accidentally pulled it out. My heart almost stopped beating. I knew I had only about five seconds before the grenade would explode. I panicked. I pulled the grenade out of my pocket and quickly tossed it far into the woods. I waited for the explosion; after ten, twenty agonizing seconds, I breathed a sigh of relief. No explosion!

It was only then that I remembered that the grenade finger had been tied down with a shoelace instead of a pin.

We reached the Ebro at dawn. Scores of small boats were carrying troops to the west side of the river. I realized that thousands of troops were involved in this operation. On one boat, an American was standing, probably because he had just gotten aboard. Someone shouted at him: "Hey, get down! Who the hell do you think you are? George Washington crossing the Delaware?"

As we crossed the river, a small fascist observation plane flew over us. Immediately hundreds of rifles fired at the plane, and it quickly disappeared.

After landing on the fascist side of the Ebro, we began marching inland. It was still very quiet. The morning dragged on. The heat became intense, as did the thirst, reminding me of Brunete. But still there was no fighting and only a smattering of rifle fire up ahead.

At about noon, we passed hundreds of fascist prisoners who had been cut off, had surrendered, and were now being taken to the rear. They seemed so young, so frightened, so helpless. They were the lucky ones, but at this moment, they didn't know it. Jim Lardner and Yale Stuart were among the Americans guarding them.

A day or two later, Sully and I were returning to the battalion position at the front. We had just finished laying a communication line from battalion headquarters to the brigade. Communication with the brigade was important; we knew that the Lincolns were to attack a fascist hill that morning.

Suddenly, we heard the front explode; we heard machine-gun fire, rifle fire, shell fire, and exploding grenades. Our men had once again gone over the top; the battle was in full swing. The closer we came to our battalion position at the front, the worse it seemed to get. Now bullets were flying over our heads. Some shells landed nearby; we fell to the ground and heard the shrapnel flying over us.

Stretcher-bearers, bent low, hurried past us. And there was Normie Berkowitz, wounded, on one stretcher. When he saw us, he gave us a big grin. "Look," he said. "I got me a blighty. Boy am I lucky!" This was the second time Normie had been hit.

I noticed that his shoes were missing. "What happened to your shoes?" I asked him.

"Aw, hell, I won't need them anymore. I gave them to Jack Shafran."

He was mistaken; he was back at the front in two weeks, and the first thing he did was to get his shoes back from Jack.

On that same hot August day, Sully and I also saw two of our comrades, Larry O'Toole and James Murphy, heading for the rear. We had always called them "the fighting Irishmen," because they were always getting into fights with other people or with each other. But they were very close, even when they got back home to the States—and they were very good soldiers. Now O'Toole was limping. He had been wounded for the third or fourth time, and Murphy was helping him to an ambulance. O'Toole asked for a cigarette; I gave him a pocketful I had just received from my sister.

When Sully and I reached the front line, we could see that things were not going well. Obviously, our attack had failed. Dozens of our men had been killed or wounded, and dozens more were still in no-man's-land, so badly wounded that they were unable to get to the rear. John Rody, a first-aid man, went out time and time again, risking his life to bring in the wounded. Miraculously, he wasn't hit.

Later that afternoon, word came that John Murra had been wounded, up at the front; he was still in no-man's-land, and it didn't look as though he would survive. Some of the men said that he was already dead.

Jack Shafran quietly announced that he was going to bring him back. He was urged to wait a few hours until it was dark, but Jack insisted on going out immediately. He crawled out, and about ninety minutes later he returned, dragging, sometimes carrying, a conscious but badly wounded John.

John was in bad shape, unable to move the bottom half of his body. John Simon, who was in charge of our first-aid men, took over. A man of small stature with a high-pitched voice, nothing mattered to Simon but taking care of the wounded and getting them safely to the rear, to the hospitals. We called him doc, but in reality he had still been attending medical school when he took his leave and became one of the first Americans to volunteer for Spain.[1]

Earlier that day, while Doc Simon was taking care of some wounded men, a shell landed near him and killed his burro, the burro that had been used to carry wounded up the road to the ambulances. When the shell landed, we had all dropped to the ground, but not Doc Simon. There he stood, in the dust, facing the fascists, shouting in his squeaky, high-pitched voice, "You dirty bastards! You killed my burro! How the hell am I going to get the wounded to the rear?"

Now he was busily attending to John Murra, who was explaining to Simon, in very detailed, medical language that even Simon seemed not to understand, just where the bullet had entered his body and what parts were damaged. He remained cool and calm, so much like a professor explaining a problem to a student. Simon told him to be quiet, to conserve his energy, and John was taken away on a stretcher.

The purpose of the attack that day had been to take Gandesa, but it had been a complete failure. The fascists had sent more and stronger forces to the area with artillery, tanks, and planes. There was no way we could have succeeded unless we had supporting forces; we just didn't have any. We were fighting with rifles, machine guns, a few pieces of artillery, and very few tanks. If our artillery sent three rounds of shells into enemy territory, the fascists would answer with a barrage of dozens of shells.

During one of the days that followed, Yale Stuart, returning to the battalion from Brigade headquarters on an ammunition truck, was caught in a shelling barrage. He was wounded by shrapnel and subsequently lost his left arm. Jim Lardner was also wounded during this action and was sent to a hospital in Barcelona.

For the next few days, we were constantly on the move. One night when Sully and I were at battalion headquarters, we were told that our companies were in a valley between two hills, one hill occupied by our side, and the other occupied by the fascists. The Lincolns were getting ready to attack the fascist hill.

By midnight the battle was intense. Sully and I could hear the artillery and grenades not too far away. When a runner from the battalion arrived and told us that Cookson wanted another transmissions man to join the men in the valley, I told Sully that I would go, because he had been volunteering for most of the tough jobs.

"Gee, thanks Harry," he exclaimed. "I'm so goddamned pooped I just must get some shut-eye."

I followed the runner, going downhill the whole way. It took half an hour to get to the men in the valley. When I got there, I felt as though I were living through a nightmare. There were dead bodies scattered everywhere. I saw about six wounded comrades waiting for first-aid men to help them up the steep hill. From other sections, I could hear cries for help and the moans of the badly wounded. The valley was pitch-black, except for the flames from the shells that landed near us. Ahead of us we could see tracer bullets sailing back and forth. The noise of the exploding shells was deafening; it continued until 3:30 in the morning.

At last, word came that the attack had been called off, and that we would have to climb back to the top of the hill where we had been originally positioned. Carrying the wounded was difficult, especially those on stretchers. I helped a young Spaniard who had a slight shoulder wound. He was very weak and leaned heavily on me, and we both walked quietly and slowly until we reached the top of the hill. It was now 5:00 in the morning, already dawn. A makeshift hospital had been set up for the many wounded.

I found a spot under a tree and fell sound asleep. When I awoke, it was late afternoon. I was given a loaf of bread and warm garbanzos. It tasted great! I finished it off with something they called coffee; I was grateful to have something—anything—to drink.

Later that evening, I sat with Normie Berkowitz, Jack Shafran, Jerry Cook, and Marty Sullivan. I told the boys that I had to go to the bottom of the hill to take a crap. There I was, with my pants down, watching a lazy burro grazing a few yards away, when a shell landed nearby. The sound of it was deafening, and the explosion knocked me down. I felt as though I had been hit with a sledgehammer. I lay there for a while, in a state of shock. Finally, I looked up and saw that the burro had been blown up into a tree and was dead. Holding my pants up with both hands, I ran through the dust up the hill to my friends. They were anxiously looking down the hill, but when they saw me they broke into hearty, relieved, laughter. "You're sure one lucky bastard!" was their comment.

On August 9 I wrote home:

> Dear kids:
>
> When you get this letter, I'll have been in Spain about a year and a half. I know how you feel about it. You feel that I ought to come home. You wonder why I don't. I explained in my letters many times. You've got to realize that when you are in the army, you can't leave whenever you want. I had two chances to go home, one last August and one in December, but I couldn't go home then with a clear conscience, so I chose to stay. I want to make it clear to you that it was my own desire to stay that caused me to stay.
>
> I hope this clears everything up. I'm just as anxious to see you and hug all of you, as you are to see me. And I have an idea that it won't be long from now. I can still see that first meal I want. You know, something light, because I'll be so nervous with joy. Two soft boiled eggs, banana with cream, and milk with cake. And later, I want that ice cream I've been thinking of for so long. And the first night home, after mom goes to sleep, I'm coming to

your house and will stay up all night talking and laughing with you. You have no idea what charm your place has for me—no, not so much your place, as just Sal, Hy, and Louise. I can just see that first night. I'm afraid my heart will swell and explode with joy. It's something to look forward to. Just think of it—to see Louise dancing, Hy drawing again, Sal ironing and cooking, Ben humming, mom baking, Pincus eating, Hickey and Vivienne holding hands, Nat day-dreaming, Jack acting. And I—just sitting in your soft chair, reading and eating crackers. That's beauty. All these things may seem small to you, but to me they are big things.

Give my love to mom and tell her that I may see her soon.

Love,

Harry

Finally, the Lincolns were taken out of that position and moved to a valley closer to the Ebro. It wasn't the safest position in the world, because the fascist planes flew over us several times a day to bomb the bridges that crossed the river. The fascists must have had a tough time bombing those bridges; because we had put up so many fake ones, it must have been difficult for them to recognize the real ones.

We spent eight days here. One man was always on guard to warn of approaching planes. When he fired his rifle, everyone was to take shelter under the trees. If anyone was seen walking or even slightly moving, there would be cries for him to keep still.

At about this time, I ran into Ed Royce, an old friend who had been among the first volunteers to come to Spain from the United States. My sister had known him very well back home and had been asking me in letters for news of him. I was never able to get any solid information on his whereabouts.

But now I learned from him that because he had been a soldier in the American army, he had been made a sergeant in Spain. In February 1937, during the battle at Jarama, the first action for the Americans, he had led his group of raw recruits over the top. Many of them had been slaughtered. Royce had been wounded, but only slightly. His mental wounds as a result of this experience were more serious. He held himself responsible for the deaths of so many of his men, and Jarama had been his first and only action until now. He had been sent to the rear for many months, where he had become an alcoholic and a drug addict. For about a year he was in and out of jail. But now, even the men in jails were being sent to the front, and Royce was among them.

Royce was glad to see me, but I immediately sensed that something was wrong.

"Harry, please get me out of here," he pleaded. "I can't take it. I'm sick."

I tried to explain to him that I was only a buck private, that I had no power to send him back to the rear, where he clearly belonged.

At that moment, the guard on duty fired his rifle to warn of approaching fascist planes. Soon the planes appeared, flying very high and off to the left of us. But their drone was loud and piercing. We hit the ground. All of a sudden, Royce screamed and ran out into the open terrain. We jumped on him and held him down. His fear was real and overwhelming, his screams ear-shattering. That same day Royce was returned to the rear, and soon after, he went home.[2]

There was an ongoing battle about three miles away from us, on a hill that was less than a mile from Gandesa. Day after day, we could see the fascist planes bombing this hill and the area around it. The bombardment went on continuously; shells landed on the hill all day and even during the night. We felt sympathy and compassion for the soldiers defending that hill. Later, we learned that the defenders were the Listers, one of the best Spanish outfits in the war.

On August 14, we were ordered back into action. We were to relieve the Listers and continue the defense of the hill known as 666 in the Sierra Pandols. This hill provided an excellent vantage point with a view that extended all the way to the Ebro. Its strategic significance was clear.

The thought of going into that inferno was frightening. We had been watching the flames of the battle, had seen ambulances coming and going with the wounded, and had listened to the continuous rumble of warfare. As we marched along a road leading to Hill 666, I had to urinate every ten minutes. Now I better understood the expression "scare the piss out of you."

As we got closer, the sound of battle got louder by the minute. I looked up at the enemy planes pounding the hill and wondered how anyone could still be alive.

This, my last action, was to be the worst by far. Again I wondered how many times I could go through a battle and not be hit.

It was dark and ominously quiet when we reached 666. We watched the Spaniards silently leaving the hill that they had held on to for more than a week. They were exhausted, and all of them seemed to be in a state of shock.

We climbed to the top of the hill carrying communications gear, machine guns, ammunition, and other equipment. It was backbreaking; we groaned and cursed, but kept going. There were no trees, no bushes, just crumbling rock and stone. It was almost impossible to dig in. Nevertheless, the companies took up positions on top of the hill. Milt Wolff, Joe Brandt, and George Watt established headquarters in a cave near the top.

The next day, the usual barrage of shells began to hit the top of the hill. Fortunately, the side of the hill where we in communications were stationed wasn't quite so bad. Once in a while a spent shell would explode near us, but compared to the infantry at the top of the hill, we were relatively safe. One time a shell exploded not too far from me, and a large piece of shrapnel landed nearby. I picked it up, then dropped it like a hot potato. Just touching it gave me a bad burn on my hand.

That evening, as the sun was setting in the West, I could see shells flying through the sunshine, seemingly floating in slow motion. How strange! I watched those silvery objects sail so gracefully, and yet I knew that in spite of their seeming beauty, they were instruments of death.

The next morning, Sully and I were asked to go to Brigade headquarters to get more equipment for transmissions. We didn't dare go via the road below; the fascists would have spotted us in a minute. We decided to go east, around the hill, and into a valley. What we saw there appeared to be a battalion at rest. Soldiers were lying all over the ground. We realized they were not "at rest"; there was an awful stench, and insects were buzzing around the men. They were all dead, as many as two hundred, very possibly soldiers from both sides.[3] Just then bullets began to fly around us, and we raced back to our hill. A little later we made a second try, and this time we did get to headquarters. We brought back lots of badly needed transmission equipment.

On our second day at Hill 666, the order came for the Lincolns to attack the enemy position on another nearby hill. We knew we were at a disadvantage; the fascists were exceedingly well equipped, and their elevated position would enable them to toss hand grenades down on our troops. The Americans were scheduled to lead the attack, and at mid-afternoon two of our batteries opened fire; our artillery began lobbing shells into their lines, and some hours later five Soviet Chatos flew above us, strafing the enemy position. The First and Third Companies of the Lincoln Battalion spearheaded the attack and suffered tremendous casualties. Aaron Lopoff, the commander of one of the companies, was hit in the head, lost his eyes, and died two days later in a hospital. A Spanish company commander also was killed. A number of men were missing, and we had to presume they were dead. Many men were wounded, some very badly. I saw Pat Roosevelt, a black comrade, crawling over the burnt rocks. When I drew closer to him, I saw that his leg had been severed; just a bit of flesh was still connecting the leg to his body. The leg was dragging along and he was bleeding profusely. I asked him to wait, told him that I'd get help. I couldn't believe it when he replied, "I'm OK," and continued crawling toward the rear. Fortunately, some first-aid men came running with a stretcher, put a tourniquet around his thigh, and carried him away to an ambulance.

Other wounded men were crawling up the hill, with still others trying to help them. It was dark, and the sights and sounds were eerie. The scene was like a bad dream. It didn't seem real, but damn it, it was.

The next day, the fascists answered with a terrible barrage, the worst I had ever seen or heard. It sounded as if thunder were crashing directly overhead. Our men on top of the hill were blown to bits. The most popular man in the battalion, Joe Bianca, commander of the machine gun company, was hit; he died a few days later.

The barrage continued hour after hour. All transmission lines were broken; we had no communication with the other companies on the hill. After a few hours of nonstop shelling and bombing, Wolff reluctantly told Sully and me to fix the lines to one of the companies. He had to be able to get word out if the fascists began an attack, as we expected they would do after this barrage.

Sully and I decided it would be easier to lay a new line rather than try to fix the old one, which must have had more than twenty breaks. Sully put a reel on his back and made a connection with the headquarter's phone. Wolff looked at us as we left the headquarters cave; he said very quietly, "I'm sorry, but it has to be done."

We started out. The scene was awful. The terrain was covered with a haze of dust; bullets flew over our heads. We wondered if anyone out there was still alive.

Sully walked ahead of me, letting the line fall from the reel he was carrying on his back. I secured the wire under the rocks on the hill, so that it would have some protection from falling shells. Suddenly a shell landed in front of Sully. The explosion was thunderous. I could see nothing but dust; the smell of gunpowder was overwhelming. I was afraid that Sully had been hit. Coughing and choking, I rushed ahead; the dust was so thick, I couldn't see my hand in front of me. Suddenly I tripped . . . over his body, scraping my hands. I felt him, but I couldn't see him.

"Sully, Sully," I pleaded. "Are you OK?"

Suddenly, the dust cleared. Sully stirred, stood up, and exclaimed: "Boy! That was a close one! Let's get on with this job."

I heaved a sigh of relief, and we continued toward what we hoped would be Company One. Shells continued to explode all around us, but Sully stayed erect, letting the line fall from the reel. I continued to secure the wire under rocks and boulders.

In a short while, we saw Alvah Bessie, commander of Company One. We quickly connected the wire to Bessie's phone, and to our great relief, he was able to reach Wolff immediately. They proceeded to have an animated talk.

My old friend Joe Rehil joined Sully and me, greeting us casually, as though we were home on a picnic.

"Hi Marty, hi Harry! How ya' doing?"

Jack Corrigan at Benicassin.
Photograph by Sam Walters.

Owen Appleton, Company Clerk, August 1937. Appleton was buried alive in his trench during a bombing at Fuentes de Ebro, October 1937.

From right: Normie Berkowitz (at machine gun); Jack Shafran; Ed Lending (with rifle). Soldiers in back unknown. Albalate del Arzobispo, September 1937. From the collection of Norman Berkowitz.

Pat Reid and Harry Fisher, near Teruel, February 1938. Abraham Lincoln Brigade Archives/Brandeis University Libraries.

A group of volunteers from Wisconsin. Front row, left to right: John Cookson, Clarence ("Slim") Kailin; back row, left to right: Fred Palmer, Harry Lichter, Ray Disch. Albacete, February 1937. From the collection of Clarence Kailin.

Ben Kasinap, medic, near Belchite, August 1937. From the collection of Norman Berkowitz.

Tom O'Flaherty, Marsa, June 1938. Abraham Lincoln Brigade
Archives/Brandeis University Libraries.

Jack Shafran reading the *Daily Worker* while convalescing in Vals
Catalonia, 35th Divisional Hospital.

Normie Berkowitz, wounded July 29, 1938, Villalba dels Arcs.
From the collection of Norman Berkowitz.

Ernest Hemingway, Hugh Slater, and Herbert Matthews, east of the Ebro, after the Retreats, April 1938. From the collection of Norman Berkowitz.

Ben Kasinap with my future wife, Ruth Goldstein, Washington DC, February 1939. From the collection of Norman Berkowitz.

Sid Rosenblatt with my sister, Sal, taken on my wedding day, May 7, 1939, New York City.

"We're OK, but how are you?"

Joe had been on the side of the hill earlier that morning when the barrage had begun. The Company One transmissions man had been killed, and Joe had volunteered to take his place. Ever since I had known Joe, I had never seen him in a serious mood, and this was no exception.

"Gee," he complained, "it's boring up here."

"What do you mean 'boring?'" Bullets were singing over our heads, and shells were still falling all around us.

"Oh, it's always the same thing. Shells exploding, sometimes bombs; bullets are always flying around, hour after hour. Boring."

A comrade close by commented: "You know the kind of boredom I would like?! Hour after hour of silence. No noise, no bullets, no shells. Just nothing. Now that's what I'd love. Real boredom."

Sully and I stayed for about half an hour to be sure the line remained intact. We sprinted back to headquarters without further incident.

The next morning, during another barrage, Milt Wolff asked Sully and me to put up yet another telephone line, this time to Company Two, Dave Smith's company. We connected the line to our headquarter's phone and then decided to lay part of the line on the side of the hill, keeping it as far from the top as we could. We hoped this would protect a good part of the line from shell fire, which was aimed at the top of the hill.

Finally, we reached the point where we had to get to the top. The shelling was intense, bullets flying all over the place. The smell of powder was strong and all around us. The ground looked black, with not a blade of grass growing.

As we hurriedly made our way to Smith's company, we passed about ten yards from a small cave. Inside, a hideous scene was taking place. Alex Pratt, the same character who had managed to alienate countless comrades, was holding a gun to the head of a very young Spanish soldier. The youngster was crying and begging Pratt not to make him go to the top of the hill. Pratt was obviously threatening to shoot him if he refused to go. "That bastard," muttered Sully. "If I had a rifle, I'd shoot *him*." Of course, gentle Sully could never have done such a thing, but I understood how he felt. Pratt was once again using the bullying tactics of our enemy, the tactics we had come to Spain to put an end to. We kept laying the transmission line and never did learn what happened to that young Spanish soldier, but the image of the scene in that cave still haunts me to this day.

Fortunately, by the time we reached Dave Smith's company, the shelling had stopped. We made the connection, and Dave was able to speak to Wolff. Our assignment to lay the line was completed. Sully and I were utterly exhausted and collapsed at the top of the hill. It felt good to get a moment's rest. Soon, Dave joined us. I lay on my back near Dave and Sully, when suddenly we heard the roar of planes coming toward us from the fascist side. There were only nine of them, flying very low in v-formation, at about two thousand feet. There we were, out in the open, with no place to take cover, no place to hide. And there was no way they could miss seeing us. I held my breath as we watched them approach. They were headed right toward our hill, coming straight at us. The bomb-bay doors were open. I thought surely these were my last seconds on earth. Dave and Sully seemed calm; my heart was pounding. I knew that if the bombs started to fall when the planes were still hundreds of yards away, we'd be dead. But the planes continued their flight, and when they were directly overhead, I knew we were safe. We watched the bombs drop only seconds after they passed us. We learned later that the bombs were aimed at the British battalion, in reserve about a mile south of us. Fortunately, that bombing did very little damage, and the British sustained few casualties.

The battalion remained on this hill for about ten days; the bombing and shelling were constant. Nevertheless, Sully and I made numerous trips laying or fixing lines to the different companies.

Every now and then we would have prominent people visit us at Hill 666. Ernst Toller, the famous German playwright, and Joe North of the *Daily Worker* spent time with us. One day a car stopped at the foot of the hill. Bullets flew all around it. Two men got out of the car and started running up the hill. They climbed frantically and laboriously until they reached our resting place; they were exhausted. The two men were Herbert Matthews and Ernest Hemingway. I admired them, coming into this dangerous part of the world, risking their lives to get a story.

The day finally came when we were relieved by a Spanish outfit. We were a bunch of zombies when we left—spiritless, tired, looking like the exhausted Listers we had relieved ten days earlier.

Our next position was a good distance from Hill 666, still on the same side of the Ebro, but quiet and out of earshot of the sounds of war. Here we rested, talked, wrote letters, read old newspapers, and just waited for the next action. John Power joined us one day. John and I had been runners for Company One commander Paul Burns when we had gone over the top at Mosquito Hill. John had been wounded there, and it had been over a year since I had last seen him. Later he joined the British Battalion, and now he was a company commander with the rank of captain. After the hugging and handshaking were over, he said he was happy to see me still with the Lincoln Battalion. So many of the comrades had been killed, or had been wounded and gone home. He sat with us and joined in our bull session. Afterward, he expressed surprise at the bitching and griping by some of the Americans. I assured him that in spite of their complaining, they were terrific soldiers and good comrades. They bitched only when they were in the rear. I didn't have the heart to tell him that I was one of the best gripers in the battalion.

That was the last time I saw John Power. He returned to Ireland after the withdrawal of the International Brigades from Spain.

While we were in this rest position we learned from an article by Herbert Matthews in the *New York Times* that the International Brigades would soon be withdrawn from Spain. Shortly thereafter, Commander Wolff told me that I was going on leave to Paris for a week or so, and that I should be ready to head out in two hours. This seemed strange, because the border to France was open only to those leaving Spain permanently; to get back I'd have to climb the Pyrenees again. I looked at Wolff quizzically. He smiled at me and winked, and I knew that I was on my way home.

I was to be one of seven Americans, all of whom had been in action from the earliest days, to be in this first group to leave Spain. I knew that we would not be returning; the Internationals were indeed leaving Spain.

It was very difficult to say good-bye to my comrades.

Marty Sullivan said, "I'll miss you, but I'm glad you're going. You deserve it. Write to me." We shook hands and parted. I walked away quickly, because I knew I was about to burst into tears.

Saying good-bye to Joe Rehil was no easier. Joe, as usual, wise-cracked, but at the last moment became serious, hugged me, and said how glad he was that I was leaving Spain in one piece. Jack Shafran and Jerry Cook pounded me on the back, genuinely happy for me. Jack made me promise to say hello to Ruthie Goldstein, an organizer for our union. (I not only said "hello," I decided I wanted to spend the rest of my life with her. We were married eight months later.)

When I said good-bye to Cookson, commander of my transmissions group, he promised to visit me as soon as he returned to the States. He never did. He was killed about three weeks later, when the Americans were unexpectedly sent to the front when our lines were broken.

I couldn't know it then, but there were to be many years of close friendship after the war with John Murra, Jack Shafran, Jerry Cook, Normie Berkowitz, Ed Rolfe, Charlie Nusser, Ralph Fasanella, Leon Tenor, Irv Fajans, Hy Stone, Dave Engels, John Rody, and Lenny Lamb. But so many others were gone.

I remembered Max Krauthamer, Mel Offsink, and Jack Shirai, sitting with a large group of comrades talking about the restaurant they were going to open in New York after the war, about how the Americans who fought in Spain would never have to pay for a meal there. All three died in Spain.

I thought about Butch Entin, my close friend during the department store strikes back home, with whom I had spent many a night in jail, a man who had risked his life protecting a young mother with her baby in her arms when a cop tried to molest her on a freight train outside Gary, Indiana. He died at Brunete.

I could still see Steve Nelson trying to persuade Oliver Law, the first black commander of American troops, not to lead the attack on Mosquito Hill, and Commander Law explaining that he had to lead the men if he expected them to go into battle. He did, and died an hour later.

I had become so close to Jack Corrigan, the comrade who had climbed the Eternal Light flagpole in New York to raise the "Free Ernst Thaelmann" banner. He and another comrade had volunteered to man a machine gun against the advancing fascists during the retreats so others could escape. Neither was seen again.

Rudy Haber looked even younger than his nineteen years when he joined us near Caspe during the retreats. The fascists were less than half a mile away. I saw young Haber tell a Spanish lieutenant that he would stay with him and feed the machine gun. Both were killed.

Then there was Dave Reiss, the pacifist from New Jersey, who led his men on a search for fascists with nothing more than a few rifles and machine guns. He too was killed during the retreats.

I remembered Lou Cohen, with whom I had carried the furniture of evicted families back up to their apartments in New York. I sat with him one day in Spain while he told me the horror of seeing his comrades, wounded and dead, crushed by an Italian tank in Caspe. He died the day after we spoke.

I recalled the wonderful discussions led by Aaron Lopoff and his friend Alvah Bessie whenever there was a lull during the retreats. These talks would take our thoughts away from the nightmares surrounding us—which was surely the aim those two great guys had in mind. Lopoff led a difficult attack on a fascist position in the Sierra Pandols and was blinded. He died a few days later.

How could I ever forget Tom O'Flaherty, who could have put me to sleep in a matter of seconds after I picked a fight with him? I tried my best to hurt him but barely even touched him. He tried his best to do nothing more than barely touch me. What a gentle fellow he was. He was killed during our last offensive across the Ebro River while on a scouting mission.

Sid Rosenblatt did return home in 1939, but was no longer the carefree fellow I had known. He had changed in Spain, particularly after the tragic events at the Hermitage, where he had cradled his dying friend, Dave Reiss, refusing to leave him even as the fascists closed in. Sid was captured that day and spent a year in one of Franco's prisons. I was delighted to have him at my wedding in May of 1939. But not long after that, while again fighting fascism—this time in World War II—Sid was killed in battle.

I couldn't take any more good-byes or memories. I looked at the men around me. Some were reading, others were dozing. I thought to myself, "So long, comrades. See you back at home." We weren't going to win this war, that was clear by now. But there had been a purpose to our fight, and that was what had given us our strength. Otherwise, the war would have been an unending horror, a tragic waste of precious life. But Spain's struggle was a different kind of war—a people's fight for its democratic rights. I felt proud to have been part of the International volunteer army that had come to help Spain put an end to fascism.

12. Home

OUR SMALL GROUP OF SEVEN MEN finally arrived at a camp near Barcelona. I was numb. My thoughts were still with the comrades I had left behind, and I felt a wrenching sorrow at leaving the wonderful people of Spain, knowing all too well what their future would be.

Now I found myself in a camp filled with hundreds of Internationals—French, Germans, Czechs, Hungarians, Yugoslavs, Italians, and a few Americans. Most of these men had been badly wounded; some were blind, some had no limbs. There was very little joy here, even though everyone was preparing to return home. Some, including the Germans and Italians, could not go home.

Entertainers came to sing and dance, but the men looked straight ahead, thinking only of their families and how their lives would be different, now that they were crippled and helpless. Propaganda speeches were made, but no one listened.

I was delighted to get a day's leave to go to Barcelona and quickly headed for the hospital where John Murra was being cared for. I was glad to see him cheerful and upbeat, considering that he was paralyzed from the waist down. He didn't know if he would ever walk again. Jim Lardner and I sat at John's bedside chatting with him. Lardner had been slightly wounded in a bombing during the Ebro offensive but was returning to the battalion the next morning. John and I gave Lardner all our pesetas, because we wouldn't be needing them any more.

We never saw Lardner again. He was killed a few days later, in the last action in which the Americans participated, the same action in which John Cookson was killed.

I said good-bye to John Murra that day with a heavy heart. "I'll see you in the States, John." And with more optimism than I felt, "I expect to see you walking then; I know I won't be disappointed!"[1]

I wrote to my sister's family on September 3:

Dear kids:

At last I can write to you the good news. Before you get this letter, you should receive a cable from me from Paris. I know how happy this will make you, so you can imagine how happy I am.

Right now I'm at a rest home, not far from Barcelona. I've been here for a few days, and am beginning to feel like my old self. I'll most likely be here another week before leaving for Paris. I don't know how long I'll be in Paris, but I'll try not to stay more than a week. Less, if possible. Which means, I'll be home by the end of September or the beginning of October. If you don't get the cable, don't worry. It will be either for lack of money—or else because we're delayed. You see, we're waiting for our papers and passports, and it may take a little while to get everything straight. But I'll try to cable just as soon as I get to Paris. I know how worried you are, and I want to put an end to it. I can just imagine how happy mom will be when she hears of this.

The last letter I got from you was at brigade. I was answering the letter when I was notified to pack up. So I tore up the letter. It was the letter in which you asked me if I knew Harry Hakim. Sure I do. He's coming with me. He also came on the same boat with me.

Here is one thing I want you to do for me. Write a short note to two fellows and enclose cigarettes. One is Jerry Cook (Pat) and the other is Martin Sullivan. They are going to miss me. They'll share the cigarettes with the other boys. Sullivan is the fellow I've been closest to for the past nine months. I've promised to send him cigarettes. So till I get home, you send them. And also to Jerry.

Do you remember reading about the fellow Jack helped carry

in from no-man's land? Well, he was one of my best friends here. I visited him the other day in a hospital in Barcelona. He's coming along very nicely. He'll have to stay a few months yet. It will take him a long time till he can use his legs. He's from Chicago, but you'll meet him when he returns from Spain. He's the fellow I worked with in Albacete.

In fact, you're going to meet lots of the boys when they come back. I've been boasting about your good cooking, so you'll have to suffer the consequences. But you will like these fellows.

Nothing more for the present—except that I'm happy as hell. Get that meal ready Sal, and Louise better practice on her dancing —Let's see—Salad—2 soft eggs—bananas and cream—coffee and cake. Oh boy.

Love,
Harry

To my mother and brother I wrote:

Dear mom and Ben:

It's over a year and a half that I'm away from home now. I won't go away again for a long time. When I get back, I'm not going to do anything for the first few days, but stay home with either you or Sal and Hy. I'm not going out to any place. I'll have a lot to talk to you about. You have no idea how happy I'll be when I see you again. It seems like many years that I'm away.

I wish I had some money to buy you a good present mom, but I haven't any. By the time you get this letter, I ought to be pretty close to home.

Love,
Harry

After spending a few more days at the International Brigades camp, it was time to leave for France. The badly wounded were put on buses and ambulances; about two hundred of us walked through the town to the railroad station. The day was cold, and it was drizzling, as gloomy as could be. But our hearts were lifted when we saw that the entire village had come out to say good-bye. The people threw flowers in the street. Many fists were raised in salute. Men, women, and even the children wept openly.

The train was slow, too slow; we kept looking out of the windows for enemy planes. When we reached the station in Barcelona, we could see the devastating damage that had been done by the almost daily bombings.

As the train pulled out, a thunderous cheer went up. Here too, the people had come out to say good-bye. The train picked up speed, and soon we came to a tunnel that led into France. The train crawled through the tunnel and then slowed practically to a walking pace. It had reached the middle of the tunnel, where a white line marked the border between France and Spain. On each side of the white line were two soldiers, two Frenchmen on the French side, and two Spaniards on the Spanish side. As the train inched on, all four soldiers, both Frenchmen and Spaniards, raised their hands in a clenched-fist salute.

Soon thereafter, we emerged into the daylight of France. We left the Spanish train and then waited for several hours for a French train to take us to Paris. While waiting, the French Red Cross did its best to feed us, to make us feel comfortable and relaxed. We were given soft drinks, which actually were laxatives. Harry Hakim, sitting next to me, not knowing what that delicious drink was, kept asking for more. Finally, someone explained to Hakim that the sweet drink was very potent. Hakim was embarrassed and growled: "Why the hell did they make it taste so good!"

We had a great meal at the station restaurant. What I remember best was the banana I had after the meal; it was the first one I'd had in over a year and a half.

Later that afternoon, we boarded the train to Paris. It was covered with banners and signs, in French, explaining that this train was filled with wounded International Brigadistas who had fought against fascism in Spain.

It was early September of 1938, and the world now knew that the war in Spain was ending in a victory for Franco and fascism. The feelings in France were deep and emotional.

About an hour into our trip, the train stopped at a small city. We were amazed to see a huge crowd at the station, thousands and thousands of people, shouting anti-fascist slogans, raising their fists in salute, and singing "The Internationale." Workers and peasants had come from miles around; they threw flowers and food on the train. We were not allowed to leave the train, but we returned their salutes and joined them in singing "The Internationale."

During the night, our train stopped at more than a dozen stations. And no matter what time of night it was, thousands of people were there to greet us and to shower us with more flowers and more food. The warmth of the French people was overwhelming.

When we arrived in Paris, the depot was crowded with parents, relatives, and friends of the returning French soldiers. It was dreadful to see the pain on the faces of the French people when they saw their loved ones, some blind, some terribly crippled. But there were those who waited in vain, asking everyone who left the train if they knew their husband, son, or friend. Many had photos and were eager to show them to anyone who would stop long enough to look. The scene was heartbreaking.

The Americans—few in number—were greeted by a friendly man named Tony, who took us to a restaurant for breakfast and then put us up at a hotel. He explained that he was arranging for us to be on the *Ile de France* the next morning for our trip to New York. This was the same boat I had arrived on, so the circle was almost complete.

Now it was official. We would be home in about six days. Hakim and I went through the rest of that day as though in a dream. We were walking on clouds. I couldn't believe that I'd really be home in one week.

The next morning, Tony came to our hotel with our passports and tickets, as well as a few dollars for the little necessities on the boat.

As Hakim and I were going up the gangplank to board the liner, we were stopped by two young men, American agents, crewcuts and all. They asked us to surrender our passports. At first we indignantly refused, but when we realized we would not be allowed to leave, we gave them up with little more than a weak protest. It was almost thirty years before we were able to get passports again.

It took the *Ile de France* five or six days to cross the Atlantic. Each day seemed like a year to me.

Finally, on September 21, 1938, nineteen months after leaving New York, the *Ile de France* brought me home to New York once again.

As I ran down the gangplank, I saw my mother, my sister, Sal, and a pretty young woman with her arm around my mother. She was Ruthie Goldstein, our union organizer, who had been sent to greet me.

I was home.

Epilogue

AS I CAME DOWN THE GANGPLANK that autumn day, the worst hurricane ever to hit New York was pounding the city. Those of us returning were members of a defeated army; we had been beaten by monsters, and we knew all too well that the war we had fought was far from over. Nonetheless, I was happy. I was alive.

As the days went by, I tried to adjust to civilian life. But this became more and more difficult. Yes, I had lived through the war. But many hadn't. Half a million Spaniards had died, and I knew that many more would suffer or die at the hands of the victorious fascists. And so many of my friends had not returned, or had returned disabled physically or mentally.

My union organizer, Ruth, who had been put in charge of taking care of the union's returning soldiers, arranged social gatherings at different members' homes every Saturday night. She invited women union members to be our dates at those parties. Unfortunately, every one of the dates turned out to be a calamity; this was largely responsible for the severe depression I sank into and struggled with for some time.

My first date was a very pretty young woman. She was also very talkative, and all she wanted to talk about was the war. She wanted to know every gruesome detail and asked the stupidest questions imaginable. "How many fascists did you kill? How did it feel to kill them?" This went on for the next six or seven Saturday nights, each week with a different date. These people seemed to be thrilled by the possibility that I had killed fascists, and the more the better. But the truth was, I had no idea if I had killed even one fascist soldier. I carried a rifle only at Jarama and during the rest of the war was a runner and then a transmissions man. But this was not what they wanted to hear.

It wasn't only the women, but also many of the men—those who had not been in the war—who had this attitude. To them, war was a game. The important thing about war was how many bad guys you killed—and what a thrill it must have been to kill them!

And then there were stories in the communist *Daily Worker* about the war and about the courage exhibited by the Lincolns. Often reporters who should have known better wrote about how happy the Lincolns were to die for such a good cause, and that many died with smiles on their faces. These stories were preposterous. I saw hundreds, maybe thousands of dead bodies in Spain, and there wasn't a smiling face among them. Most of the faces revealed final moments filled with pain, horror, and fear. But no happy faces.

My first real combat action occurred during the Brunete offensive. On the second day, after we had captured Villanueva de la Cañada, hundreds of dead fascists lay on one side of the road, and many dead Loyalists, including Americans, lay on the other. As we walked past these bodies, I felt a pang of tremendous sadness to see so many young lives ended. They all looked alike, no matter which side of the road they were on. Those on the fascist side were just youngsters. They hadn't been brought up to believe in hatred, bigotry, violence, or brutality, the trademarks of the fascists—they were just kids who happened to live in territory controlled by the fascists, kids who would surely have preferred soccer games to war. I picked up one photo sticking out of the pocket of a dead fascist soldier. I still have that photo of him and his family, posing with their pet dog, and to this day, every time I look at it, that same despondent feeling I had sixty years ago overwhelms me.

But to so many Americans, even progressives, this had been a "glorious" war. And so I became depressed. Many a day, I would walk the streets of New York from morning until evening. It was almost impossible for me to eat. My sister, Sal, would force me to eat a light supper, usually of strawberries and sweet cream, and a glass of milk with some cookies. That was all, one meal a day for weeks, and even eating such a light meal was very difficult. There were times during these walks when I would be careless crossing streets and would even hope that a car would hit me and end it all.

I do not remember how long this went on, days or weeks. But I found that whenever I became disgusted with my buddies or my "dates," I would turn to Ruth, the union organizer. We would talk and take walks together, and she never once asked me how many fascists I had killed or what it felt like. Sometimes at our Saturday night parties I would fall asleep on her lap. I felt very comfortable with her and found myself liking her, then falling in love with her. While we were taking a walk in Brooklyn after one of the parties, I wanted to ask her to marry me, but I didn't know how to propose. She had met my pretty twelve-year-old niece, Louise, a few days earlier, so I asked her if she would like to be Louise's aunt. I was surprised that she said yes, and this is what ended my depression. I wanted to live again and have a family. It turned out to be the best thing that ever happened to me, and we had a wonderful life together, until her death in 1993. I'm very close to my son and daughter and my three grandchildren.

After being married to Ruth for about a year, I began telling her about Spain. We both decided that it would be a good idea to begin getting my experiences down in writing. Fortunately, my sister had saved all the letters she had received from me, so we had a beginning. Whenever possible, I made notes about things that I remembered, some sad, some gruesome, and some humorous. But something always "interfered" with the project. First John was born; then I was in the war that some of my letters predicted would occur; then Wendy was born. We were also so fascinated by or involved in political events—the civil rights movement, the anti–Vietnam War movement, events in Cuba, Chile, Nicaragua, and elsewhere, the assassinations of the Kennedys, Martin Luther King Jr., and Malcolm X—that we just couldn't get our minds on the project. It wasn't until the late 1980s that we finally began to work on it in a disciplined fashion. Ruthie conducted interviews with some of the vets, and we got busy writing. We were in the process of editing the manuscript when we learned that Ruthie had cancer. Once again we stopped working. It wasn't until two years after Ruthie died that I was able to begin working again, adding some material and making necessary changes.

In 1986 the International Brigades decided to have a reunion in Spain to commemorate the fiftieth anniversary of the beginning of the war. Ruthie, John, John's wife, Dena, and I joined about a hundred Lincoln vets and several hundred more veterans from other countries. We visited the Jarama and Brunete battlefields and found it very interesting, but there was only one affair held in Madrid that the *people* of Spain were invited to. Most of the Spanish people did not know about our coming, because the Spanish government intentionally kept our visit quiet. We did get messages from the socialist prime minister, but he never personally welcomed us. The mayors of Madrid, Valencia, and Barcelona each had an affair for the Brigadistas, but they did not invite any Spaniards, except government officials.

It was then about ten years since the death of Franco and the return of democracy to Spain. Naturally, under the fascist rule, the Spanish Civil War was taught in schools from the fascist point of view. And the media discussed it from the same position. In the eighties and with a socialist government it was decided to keep the war low-key, to sweep it under the rug, so to speak. The government didn't want any trouble, as they were new to power and the fascists still had some support. Only in the past few years has there been free and open discussion about the war in schools and in the media. For the first time, many young Spanish people are learning their own history, and from what we have heard here in the States, many of them are very proud that their ancestors, three generations earlier, tried to make Madrid the tomb of fascism. These young people also began learning about the role of the International Brigades—a fact that would become very clear to me in short order.

In 1995 many organizations in Spain, realizing that 1996 would be the sixtieth anniversary of the formation of the International Brigades, petitioned the government, asking them to invite the Brigadistas to return to Spain and to grant citizenship to all the living Brigadistas, about 750 of us. There was great enthusiasm for this—even the king supported it. More surprisingly, the parliament voted unanimously in favor of this proposal. Soon after, the socialists were defeated in a general election by less than one percent of the vote, and a more conservative government came to power. Still, the new government welcomed the International Brigades and even gave money to make the trip possible for many veterans who were too poor to come on their own.

And so, in November 1996, more than 450 Brigadistas (including 73 from the United States) and over 1,200 family members and friends returned to Spain. My son and daughter, John and Wendy, their spouses, Dena and Geoffrey, and my three grandchildren, Paul, Emi, and Rachel, ages twenty-eight, thirteen, and five, also came. I was very anxious for them to see the many parts of Spain I had been in, but especially for them to meet the people of Spain. It turned out that this trip was truly the experience of a lifetime for us all. The welcome we Brigadistas and our families received from the people of Spain was heartwarming, intense, and unforgettable.

The ten days we spent in Spain were filled with receptions, rallies, parties, and discussions. We were treated to concerts, art exhibitions, and countless other cultural events. Veterans toured Madrid, Barcelona, Seville, Albacete, Guernica, and dozens of other large cities and small towns. We visited our old training bases and some battle fronts. But most important, we met with the Spanish people. The older people greeted us with tears and remembrances. The younger people greeted us with enormous respect, admiration, and questions—so many questions from the young!

One town we visited was Alcorcon, a modern suburb of Madrid. Our bus entered a schoolyard filled with children waving and smiling. We were taken to a modern gymnasium, where tables were set for a feast. And a feast it was. Most of the seven or so American Brigadistas present sat at one table, but my family and I sat at another with three town officials. Fortunately, my daughter-in-law, Dena, was able to translate back and forth. We learned that one man, an assistant mayor, was a communist; another, in charge of cultural affairs, was a socialist; and the third representative was a republican, more or less our equivalent of a liberal democrat.

We ate and ate and had a lovely time. My granddaughters, Emi and

Rachel, were invited into a third-grade classroom after the meal, something they will always remember. And when the officials heard that my son, John, plays the guitar, they found one for him so he could sing a few Spanish Civil War songs.

A little while later, dozens of high school students joined us in the gym. One student made a speech welcoming us and thanking us for helping their ancestors fight against the fascists. Then the teenagers gathered around me and the other Brigadistas asking questions in broken English and trying to figure out our answers in broken Spanish. By now, Emi was talking to some girls her age, and other teenagers seemed to be waiting in line for their turn to hug and kiss little Rachel. Some of the students asked John, who was still holding the guitar that had magically appeared, if he would sing Beatles songs. He was happy to oblige.

One student, about sixteen years old, stayed with me for a very long time. He wanted to know what had motivated us Americans to come from such a rich country to fight with the poor people of Spain. I explained that most of the people of my country were also poor at that time, but more important, that we were strongly anti-fascist. And we were so proud of the Spanish people for being the first to stand up to the fascists.

As we lined up for photos and prepared to leave the school, the mayor came over to each Brigadista and each family member and presented us with lovely gifts—shoulder bags, books, bronze key chains, pens, printed proclamations, and so much more. I told the assistant mayor that I was surprised we were remembered sixty years after the war. His response was that the people of Spain would remember us "sixty hundred years from now."

Then we walked a few blocks to the town's cultural center. As we entered the building, music of the International Brigades was playing. Most of the group sat in the pleasant cafeteria and sipped lemonade, but our luncheon host, the minister of culture, took my family on a tour of the building, first to his office, where he gave Emi and Rachel more gifts, then to show us exhibits of photos, paintings, and sculptures. He then took us high up on a catwalk, where we watched the Russian National Opera rehearse *La Traviata*. When it was time for us to board the bus, our new friend hugged and kissed us all, with tears in his eyes.

I fell asleep on the bus, thinking I'd wake up back at the hotel. But instead I was awakened by Geoffrey shaking me. "Look out the window," he said. A police escort had joined us as our bus negotiated its way through crowded streets. We arrived at a music conservatory, where hundreds of people were waiting to greet us. They gave flowers to each of the Americans, including the children. We entered a packed auditorium where hundreds more people cheered wildly. Everybody was trying to get near the aisle, to see us better and to grab our hands. Many people, especially the older ones, were crying. One older couple approached me, stopped me in the aisle, and kissed me on both cheeks.

When things quieted down, we were treated to a beautiful concert by a youth orchestra and a youth band. It was moving and wonderfully entertaining. Another reception then followed the entertainment.

The next day there was to be a large reception in Albacete. My family was spending the night in a hotel about an hour outside the city, and headed out to the gathering in two cars. We noticed on the map that about halfway between our hotel and Albacete was a place I was most anxious to visit—the town of Madrigueras, where a very special family had cared for me while I was in training.

The town had been tiny in 1937, and as we were to discover, it hadn't changed much. We had to get off the main highway and take old dirt roads quite a few miles into the hinterlands. When we asked for directions, perhaps ten miles outside Madrigueras, locals couldn't help us, because they had never heard of the place. Finally, a policeman gave us instructions, and we drove into the town, narrowly avoiding the young man riding his burro in the roadway. I had warned my family that this was the smallest place we would visit, and that unlike Madrid or Alcorcon the people here were not likely to remember us or even know anything about us, after sixty years.

Geoff and John parked the cars near a church. I got out and asked two elderly people if they remembered the International Brigades. Both shrugged their shoulders, perhaps not understanding my poor Spanish. My assumption was that they simply knew nothing about us. I suggested to my family that we continue on to Albacete, that there was no point in staying here in Madrigueras.

Just then, Wendy ran over to me and said, "I have something to show you, Dad. I don't think they've forgotten." We walked around the corner and there, on a nondescript building, was a twelve-foot, handwritten banner that read in part, "Bienvenidos Camaradas Brigadistas," words that made the rest of the banner's message entirely clear.

Upon closer investigation, we realized that the banner was hanging on the local Communist Party headquarters. It was Friday evening, and the building was deserted. I asked a passerby where the communists were. His response: "They're all in church." (I couldn't help thinking how much times had changed!)

Geoffrey went into the church, and a moment later came running out, saying a young man had something to show me. We all entered the church. The young man told us to follow him, and he led us to the rear of the church, where the floor was strewn with old pipes and cartons and all kinds of junk. He took a ladder out of a closet, propped it up against the wall, and ushered us up. It was a bit difficult for me at the age of eighty-five to climb that rickety ladder, but some strong hands helped me and I made it. About fifteen young Spaniards followed me and my family up the ladder. It was dark, except for the light from a flashlight that we followed to a small room at the end of the hall. There our guide set up some construction lights to illuminate the walls of the room, walls that were covered with graffiti written by members of the International Brigades sixty years before. "No pasarán," "Abajo fascismo," "Red Front," some words printed in English, some in German and Spanish. Drawings of clenched fists. Poems to girlfriends.

Apparently, this room and one other had actually been a Spanish Loyalist prison for those who had committed minor offenses—drunkenness, for example. And while the men were held here, for a matter of days usually, they left their mark. We were told that when Franco won the war, he had ordered all left-wing graffiti to be destroyed, and had sent crews throughout the country to obliterate all such writings. But for decades the people of Madrigueras had hidden these rooms; they destroyed the stairway to the second floor and piled garbage all around. Just possibly this tiny church in this tiny town is now the home of the only extant graffiti scrawled by members of the International Brigades.

When we climbed down the ladder to the main part of the church, there were several dozen people milling around. An elderly woman approached me, anxious to talk. It seems she had been a ten-year-old girl when the Americans were there in 1937. Through an English-speaking translator, the woman told us how clearly she remembered the Americans, the candy we gave to them, the games we played with them, the simple magic tricks we performed. Then she told me what happened after the war. Germans entered the town, arrested the top officials, and shot them. And for months afterward, the people of Madrigueras were severely punished for having helped the Internationals. Shipments of food to the town were stopped, and many, perhaps a third of the townspeople, starved to death. I couldn't help but wonder what happened to the family that had "adopted" me, that had fed me so well, but unfortunately I couldn't tell the woman the family name or address. After sixty years I simply can't remember. It broke my heart to think that their kindness to me may have been their death sentences.

About this time a busload of British Brigadistas arrived, along with several Swiss veterans. One Brigadista from Switzerland was in a wheelchair. I approached him, introduced myself, and put out my hand to shake his. He had difficulty raising his hand to mine, and I noticed that three of his fingers were missing. He looked in my eyes and quietly said just one word: "Teruel."[1]

My thoughts were interrupted by a group of young men who shyly approached me with something in their hands. It was the banner that had been hanging on the Communist Party building. They presented it to me as a gift, from the young people of Madrigueras.

After several hours of fascinating and sometimes heartbreaking discussions, my family started to head to our cars. A young woman came rushing over and asked me not to leave yet, explaining that she was a representative from town hall and had something for me. She left and returned moments later with three beautifully packaged bottles of Madrigueras wine and a box containing six elegant knives. On this box there is a silver plaque, thanking the Brigadistas for fighting for the freedom of Madrigueras. She also gave me a proclamation issued by the town government, making all Brigadistas "adopted sons" of Madrigueras.

Now I was an adopted son not only of one Madrigueras family, but of the whole town.

As my family got into our two cars, a most moving thing occurred. A group of young people lined the street and stood silently with clenched-fist salutes. We drove off in tears. But the silence was soon broken as a group of older women began running along the side of my car, crying and throwing kisses. It was a send-off that brought me back sixty years to that day when forty of us were leaving Madrigueras for the Jarama front. In the wee hours of the morning, while still completely dark, practically the whole town had surrounded our two trucks, giving us food, and crying as we headed off. Then, too, many had silently raised their clenched fists in salute.

The next day we headed out, in the general direction of Barcelona. We made a brief stop in Teruel, eating lunch in a nice restaurant, but my mind was not on food. I was recalling events of sixty years earlier, particularly of the day in Teruel when a large number of German planes had circled overhead, preparing to bomb us. Suddenly a small group of Russian fighter planes had appeared and scared the German bombers off. We witnessed a dogfight between the Soviet and German fighter planes in the distance, each losing a few aircraft. We were all grateful to the Soviet pilots, many of whom lost their lives while protecting us.

In 1979 Ruth and I were invited to visit the Soviet Union. One of the things we did was to visit the office of the Soviet veterans who had fought in Spain as pilots, tankists, or advisers. A Soviet general, then in his seventies and retired, approached me and asked what fronts I had been at in Spain. After naming a few, I mentioned Teruel. He became very excited and told me that he had flown over Teruel at the time I was there. He put his arms around me in a great bear hug, and kissed me on both cheeks and then on the lips. I told the general that this was the first time in my life I had ever been kissed by a general. He laughed and kissed me again.

My return to Spain was an emotional roller coaster—warm welcomes, happy reunions, fascinating conversations, but also bitter memories. A brief visit to Belchite was particularly painful. It was here that the Germans tested dive-bombing techniques, destroying the city. When Franco won the war, he decided to keep Belchite in ruins as a lesson to the people, to show them what happens when a population opposes fascism. Today, the city is still in ruins, with remnants of that earlier destruction still strewn over the landscape. (Now, busloads of tourists come from all over the world to see what fascism did to its own people.) But we had a wonderful experience when a late-evening stop in Albacete led us to an exhibition of international memorabilia from the war—letters, photos, books, artwork, postage stamps, and more. (We arrived as the center was closing, but when the director learned that I was a Brigadista, he reopened the halls and gave us a personally guided tour.) And our Spanish journey was also laced with a bit of magic, as our day in the Sierra Pandols proved.

I wanted to show my family one battle site in the mountains near Gandesa. It was early Sunday morning, and again our two-car caravan made its way along unfamiliar roads, now in mountainous territory. I had forgotten how extensive the Sierra Pandols were, and had no idea whether I'd be able to pick out the hill known as 666.

As we drove, we discussed the possibility of finding a guide in Gandesa, or at least asking directions to the hill. But would anyone even know what we were talking about? Would anyone remember?

We pulled into Gandesa. Not a soul to be seen. Was everyone in church, or just sleeping late? Up the road we saw a sign for a restaurant. Because we hadn't eaten breakfast yet, we decided to get something to eat and hoped there would be someone in the diner who could help us. As we headed up the road toward the restaurant, I began to feel a bit hopeful that we'd find 666. But I also expressed some regret that if we did find it, I wouldn't be visiting it with two special people—Milt Wolff, who had been our commander during the battle, and a writer I had been introduced to back in the States, Eunice Lipton, whose uncle, Dave Lipton, had been killed here.

We pulled into the restaurant parking lot, which was empty except for a somewhat incongruous tour bus. Geoff pulled up next to the bus, and who should be standing there but Milt Wolff! "What the hell are you doing here, Harry?" he shouted as I got out of the car, both of us delighted and amazed.

Milt was there with a group of American graduate students whose professor had hired a guide to take them to Hill 666. Milt invited us to join them and told me he wanted me to meet someone who had already boarded the bus—a writer from the States named Eunice Lipton! It was a terrific reunion for me and made the upcoming trek all the more meaningful.

I climbed on the bus and was greeted by the young students. Milt and I took turns speaking to them about this battle and the site they were about to visit, as the bus led the cars up a big hill. Finally, the bus could go no farther on the winding, gravelly road, so the students piled into a waiting cart, which was then pulled up the hill by a farmer in a tractor. The little cars followed. Finally, we all left our vehicles and trudged the last mile or so to a point as close to the actual battle site as we could get. This was very rough terrain, as I remembered. But I also remembered, with startling clarity, the days I had spent there sixty years earlier.

It was on 666 that a man we thought indestructible, Joe Bianca, was blown about twenty feet into the air by a shell. His body seemed to float in slow motion. He died soon after. It was also here that I saw Pat Roosevelt, a black comrade, crawling on this rocky hill with his leg practically blown off, bleeding profusely, but refusing help until others whom he considered more seriously wounded could be tended to. It was on Hill 666 that I saw Alvah Bessie desperately trying to help his friend, Aaron Lopoff, who had lost both his eyes and who died a few days later. It was in this area that my friend John Cookson, a mathematics instructor and a graduate student at the University of Wisconsin, was killed. Jim Lardner was killed near here as well. And so many more. It was a difficult time for me, remembering all those people, all those events. The memories were terrible.

We finally made our way back to the cars and the tractor and headed up to an even higher point on the mountain; from here it seemed one could see the entire Spanish landscape. It was a spectacular view, offset only by the knowledge that a terrible event had taken place so nearby. A dramatic monument stands at this site in memory of all those who died at the battle for Hill 666.

Finally, emotionally drained, we left Gandesa and started our trek to Barcelona, stopping for a quick look at Mora de Ebro, very near the bridge where we ended the retreats. It brought back memories of crossing the bridge before it was blown up. After we crossed, people had to swim the wide, fast-flowing river. Whenever another survivor showed up on our side of the water, he would be met with hugs and tears of joy. But it was also here that four of my friends, Sid Rosenblatt, Charles Keith, Leon Tenor, and Hy Wallach, were taken prisoner.

Our next scheduled event was in Barcelona. It was a stormy evening, with torrential rain, dramatic lightning, and gusty winds. A rally was to take place at a sporto palace that seated eight thousand people. In spite of the weather, the arena was jammed and full of electricity. Over five hundred young communists from various countries attended and got the place jumping, quite literally. They sang all the old songs, and most of the eight thousand people, including the old Brigadistas, joined them. They sang "The Internationale" about a dozen times and chanted the words "no pasarán" until the hall seemed to shake. In an odd way, it reminded me of another incident that took place almost sixty years earlier.

I was in Madrid, on leave from the Lincolns, and for the first time in months, was enjoying a night's sleep in a real bed in a hotel. It was so comfortable that one morning, when the sirens sounded a warning of incoming German planes, it was impossible for me to get out of bed. The bombs started falling, and once again I wondered if I'd survive. The noise was terrible. But through the noise, I could hear something even louder than the falling bombs —hundreds of people in the streets below singing "The Internationale." When the bombing was over, the people began shouting, "¡No pasarán! ¡No pasarán!" And I lay in bed and listened. Now, three generations later, I was hearing those words again, shouted with the same spirit and fervor.

At the end of the rally, people were asked to remain in the arena until the Brigadistas had left. The Spanish people crowded near the aisles to applaud as we walked out. One couple approached me and said that they had traveled two hundred miles to come to this event. Other people took my hands and said, simply, "Gracias, gracias." And indeed, those were the words I heard again and again and again during my return to Spain. And the same words were said to the people of Spain, in English, German, Russian, Italian, French, and many other languages—the languages of the International Brigades—as *we* thanked *them* for taking their stand against the evil that is fascism.

Notes

1. THE GREAT DEPRESSION

1. One young man, Lou Cohen, worked with us on weekends. During the week he was employed as a bookkeeper. I remember Lou as a very sensitive fellow who often had tears in his eyes when he saw the despair of the evicted families. He was also a slightly built fellow like me, and so we often trudged up and down the stairs together. Many years later, in 1938, I met Lou again, in Spain. Two days after our reunion, he was killed in battle.

2. Years after my involvement with Commonwealth but before it was destroyed, Orval Faubus was a student there and became president of the student body. In 1957, as governor of Arkansas, he gained notoriety when he actively resisted the federal desegregation of Little Rock's public schools. Later, when running for a second term as governor, the opposition dug up his history at Commonwealth. Though Faubus admitted attending the school, he claimed not to have known it was radical. But the opposition presented photographs taken at the time Faubus was student body president—with pictures of Joseph Stalin, V. I. Lenin, Eugene Debs, Norman Thomas, and Earl Browder on the walls of the school. Needless to say, Faubus was defeated in that election.

3. Another time, at the height of the Depression, Butch and I were riding the freights. Somewhere in Indiana, the train was stopped by the railroad cops (also known as "bulls"), and about fifty of us freight riders were lined up and searched. The cops kept their pistols and rifles pointed at us, cursing and threatening to shoot. One of the freight riders was a

young woman with a very young child in her arms. When one of the cops waved his pistol at her and made obscene remarks, Butch intervened and warned the bull to be more respectful.

"Where the hell are you from?" the cop asked.

"From the Bronx in New York."

"Oh, you're one of those goddamn lousy Jew-boys from New York, you son of a bitch."

Butch just looked at him and said, "Why don't you put that gun away and let's fight it out. You're nothing but a goddamn coward, or you wouldn't be picking on a defenseless woman."

The railroad cop responded by pointing his pistol directly at Butch's head, threatening to pull the trigger.

I wanted to apologize for Butch, but I couldn't get the words out of my mouth.

Butch just looked him in the eye, not saying a word, and not flinching. Just then another cop came over and told the bull to put his gun away, and not to be such a jerk. I breathed a sigh of relief and pulled Butch away.

2. THE THREAT OF FASCISM

1. Ernst Thaelmann was the head of Germany's Communist Party at the time. He was later killed by the Nazis.

2. I never did live up to this promise, but I often wondered if I was confusing my letter readers back home. The weather in Spain turned out to be so bad so much of the time—bitter cold, blistering hot, blizzards, and so forth—that it wouldn't have made much sense to say that the weather was lovely. The censors surely would have picked up on this incongruity. Anyway, things were almost never going well for us . . . but why should I have worried everyone back home even more than they already were?

3. SPAIN

1. Herman Bottcher was stripped of his U.S. citizenship because of his participation in the Spanish Civil War. Nonetheless, he volunteered for the U.S. Army when World War II broke out and eventually became one of America's most famous heroes in the Pacific arena. By a special act of Congress, his citizenship was reinstated so that he could be made a cap-

tain. He was awarded the Distinguished Service Cross and Bronze Oak Leaf Cluster for extraordinary heroism in action near Buna, New Guinea.

Pat Reid's influence on Bottcher was enormous. In spite of his strong belief in discipline, Bottcher broke one of the cardinal rules of the U.S. Army during World War II by refusing to live with officers. He socialized only with enlisted men.

2. Ironically, Johnson had been one of those thought to be a government agent while aboard the *Ile de France,* always openly reading communist literature, and getting into "dangerous" political conversations. Word had gotten around to keep away from him, and so we had. How embarrassed we were later to discover that he was in charge of training the Americans at Figueras.

3. Marion Merriman rushed to Spain when word arrived that her husband had been wounded. She stayed in Spain for many months and was made a corporal in the Abraham Lincoln Battalion. Robert Merriman had not been seriously wounded, but he was killed in a later action. Marion Merriman tells her story in her book, *American Commander in Spain: Robert Hale Merriman and the Abraham Lincoln Brigade.*

4. JARAMA

1. I never did see fascists surrendering as I wrote in these letters. I believed stories others told me. I do remember the leaflets.

2. The "Slim" I mention in this letter was Clarence Kailin from Wisconsin.

5. BRUNETE

1. Months later, John returned to the front, this time as company commander of the British battalion. Interestingly, at the time I had arrived at Jarama, a large percentage of Lincolns were Irish, some from the United States and many from Ireland. The men from Ireland did not want to fight with the English, preferring to fight with the Americans. But after a while, I suppose in the spirit of unity, the English and the Irish got together and formed one British battalion. Many of the Irish in that battalion became officers, and I understand that they got along very well with the English.

2. Usera was sent to the rear, and then back to the States. About fif-

teen years later, when Milt Wolff testified as an unfriendly witness before a Washington congressional committee, he ran into Usera. Usera confided to him that he had been sent to Spain by the U.S. Army to observe and report. Perhaps that explained his strong desire to keep out of battle.

3. When my son was born in 1943, we named him John Bernard Fisher, perhaps the only child named for three Lincoln vets. ("John" was for John Murra and "Bernard" for Bernard "Butch" Entin.)

6. ALBARES

1. Many years later, one of these wonderful doctors, Edward Barsky, who was deeply loved by Spaniards, Americans, and all the Internationals, spent six months in an American jail because he would not tell the House Un-American Activities Committee the names of people who had contributed money to the families of political prisoners in Franco's jails. That congressional committee also sent several of Barsky's comrades, Ring Lardner, Jr., Lester Cole (both of the Hollywood Ten), and Dr. Jacob Auslander, to a federal prison in Danbury, Connecticut, for refusing to name names. A short time later, Congressman J. Parnell Thomas, a Republican from New Jersey and chairman of that congressional committee, was convicted of putting no-show employees on the federal payroll and then pocketing their salaries. He arrived in handcuffs at the same federal prison in Danbury to serve time alongside three of the men he had had convicted.

7. BELCHITE

1. Many of her letters said this; of course, there was no maidl. But, as fate would have it, one very special maidl (my future wife, Ruthie, a representative sent by the union to welcome us home) was at dockside when the *Ile de France* brought me home from the war. How convenient for my mother!

8. TARAZONA

1. Sadly, as we were to discover, Butch had been killed near Brunete.

2. Johnson never again came to the gymnasium, and that was the last we ever heard about that incident.

3. Appleton was killed soon after this at Fuentes, while in a trench, during a bombing. The trench was hit, and he was buried in it.

9. TERUEL

1. When Sullivan returned to the States, he couldn't stay away from liquor. He left his wife and stayed in New York's Bowery. The Veterans of the Abraham Lincoln Brigade twice got him into a hospital, but both times he left and returned to the streets. In the late fifties, Sullivan's body was found in a gutter in the Bowery.

2. One day, Earl Browder was having a session with some American officers. They were meeting in a cabin, and a soldier was guarding the door. One fellow, a Brooklynite named Lou Secundy, wanted to see Browder, as apparently they had known each other back home quite well. Secundy asked the guard to let him in, as he and "Oil" were good friends. The guard, a Midwesterner, asked Secundy why he referred to Browder as "Oil." "I always call him by his 'foist' name," responded Secundy. The guard let him in.

3. I learned later that Corrigan was killed when his company was ordered to retreat quickly because the fascists were closing in on them. He and a friend of his, Paul MacEachron, a student from Oberlin College in Ohio, volunteered to hold the fascists back while the rest of the company got a good start. They were never seen again.

10. RETREATS

1. Yale was mistaken about one thing: He wasn't the only survivor. It wasn't until the spring of 1939, when Sid Rosenblatt was freed after more than a year as a war prisoner, that I learned the full story of what happened that day. About fifteen minutes after Sully and I left the Hermitage, things quieted down. Reiss, Parker, and some others went outside to see what was going on. Just at that moment, as Yale had told us, a shell or a bomb landed outside the cave, right where the Americans were standing. Parker and others were killed immediately, and others were badly wounded. Sid, hearing the explosion, rushed out of the Hermitage and saw so many dead and injured. He rushed to Dave Reiss, who was soaked in blood, able only to whisper. According to Sid, only a

few words came from Dave, that it was no use trying to save him, that he was dying. Then Dave stopped whispering. Blood was coming through his clothes in his midsection. Sid opened his jacket and shirt, and what he saw made him sick. Dave's insides were literally falling out. Sid tried to put Dave's guts back into his body in a vain attempt to save him. Dave stared at Sid, his eyes wide open with a questioning look as though asking, "What happened, what's going on?" Sid began to cry and held onto Dave's hands. And Dave, with his eyes wide open, still focused on Sid.

Finally, Yale Stuart told Sid to run. Fascist tanks were approaching. Yale and others rushed in the direction of Belchite, but Sid just held on to Dave's hands. Dave was dead by the time the fascists got there. And Sid became a prisoner of war.

Sid also told me an experience he had as a prisoner of war. One day, he was taken by a guard to a room with Spanish fascist officers, a few guards with rifles, and a man with a moving picture camera. Sid was told to take off his clothes. The camera began to roll and closed in on him. An officer, speaking in Spanish, pointed a stick at his penis, evidently showing that he was circumcised, as all Jews are. Everyone in the room had big grins on their faces. This film was to show that the people who were coming from other countries to fight against the fascists were Jews. All during this ordeal, Sid was enraged, but he made up his mind to take it, so that perhaps he could live to fight another day.

Sid did volunteer for the American army as soon as the United States went to war with Germany. Only after being investigated for communist activities and for fighting in Spain was he finally allowed to go to the front in Europe. He was killed there as an infantryman.

2. I wondered what would have happened if we had had artillery and anti-aircraft guns on the hill at this time. There must have been twenty thousand or more fascist troops in the area, and hundreds of tanks and trucks. Those troops could have been routed. But it was not to be.

3. I had another experience with Ruskin when the retreats were over. One day, a huge package was delivered to me from England. I opened it, wondering who in England could have sent it. I spoke to Johnny Power, who told me that there was an Englishman named Harry Fisher who had been killed some months earlier. Johnny had known him, said he

was a good comrade, and no doubt about it, he would have wanted me to keep the package. Of course, I shared all the goodies with the men in my outfit. I didn't give it a second thought after that day. But soon after, Ruskin called me to Brigade headquarters. He demanded to know why I had opened someone else's package. I explained the circumstances, that the other Fisher had been killed. I certainly didn't think this could, or should, be considered stealing. He stared at me for a long time and then said, "I can't criticize you since you did share the package with your outfit. I believe I would have done the same thing in a similar situation."

4. About a year later, Pat visited me in the States. He stayed with my wife and me for about two weeks. That was the last time I was to see him. He died in the late forties, in Chicago, of pneumonia.

5. I met some of these British soldiers months later in our Ebro offensive; they were still fighting.

6. Cookson's closest friend, Clarence Kailin, who was a student with Cookson at the University of Wisconsin, wrote a book about him some time later. I was impressed by the fact that Cookson, as a mathematics instructor at the university, had written a letter to Albert Einstein about an error Einstein had made in a complicated math equation. Einstein wrote back to Cookson, thanking him for correcting his mistake.

7. Early in 1937, many Americans and others tried to reach Barcelona via a ship named *The City of Barcelona*. The ship was hit and sunk by the Italians and many of its passengers were killed. Benny Kasinap told the story that while swimming in the water without a life preserver, he saw an elderly man with one. He told everyone that he took the life preserver from the old man to save himself. Naturally, the comrades were aghast. "How the hell could you do such a thing?" we all asked. His answer was that he had actually helped the war effort. He had taken a life preserver from a man who was too old to fight, and saved his own life so he could help save democracy. He made plenty of enemies with that story. But the truth, according to others on *The City of Barcelona,* was that Benny was actually selfless and courageous that day. I was told that he was an excellent swimmer and was responsible for saving a number of lives. And because my memories of him as a first-aid man during the attack on Mosquito Hill are very positive—I remember him going out

into no-man's-land to bring in many wounded—I tend to believe the witnesses' stories, not his own.

8. Early in July, I was given a two-day pass for Barcelona. Pat Reid was in Barcelona at the time, waiting to go home, so we arranged, via letters, to meet there. The fascists were bombing the city heavily, and air-raid sirens were constantly shrieking. At the sound of the air-raid sirens, the streets would empty. But Pat just ignored them, so, of course, I did. I kept urging Pat to get into a shelter, but he wouldn't hear of it. Fortunately, the bombs never landed near us.

The thing I remember most about Barcelona was that restaurant. You could get in only by saying a password to a guard, and Pat knew the password. The restaurant was owned by a Jewish couple. Pat told me they were Trotskyites. I didn't care, because the food was homemade and typically Jewish. It started with gefilte fish and chicken soup, then was followed by chicken, baked potato, peas, salad, apple pie, strudel, and tea. I remember that we even ordered a second portion and finished it. I felt so at home. It was the best food I ate my entire time in Spain.

9. Tom had actually been the Golden Gloves champion of North Carolina. Before coming to Spain he had become a professional boxer.

10. Jim Lardner was killed at the end of the war, during the Ebro offensive. Jim's older brother, Ring Lardner Jr., became involved with the Veterans of the Abraham Lincoln Brigade and has remained friendly with that organization for decades. In the fifties, he was blacklisted as one of the Hollywood Ten and served almost ten months in jail for standing by his principles. Later, he wrote the popular movie *M*A*S*H,* and in 1970 won an Oscar for best adapted screenplay.

11. For decades, whenever I tried to recall the name of the lieutenant who had ordered me to kill Abramofsky, I couldn't remember it. I'm sure I had somehow blocked him from my memory. It was at a New York hotel where the veterans were holding their annual dinner some thirty years later that a man approached me and asked if I remembered him.

"You look familiar, but I can't recall your name."

"I'm Paul Blake. Don't you remember when I asked you to shoot that deserter?"

I stared at him for a few seconds, dumbfounded. Then I said some four-letter words to him and walked away.

12. In 1994 a novel was published about the Americans' experiences in the Spanish war. This book, *Another Hill,* was written by Milton Wolff, who was the last of the eleven men to command the Lincolns during the war. I had looked forward to reading Milt's book for some time—and got the shock of my life when I did. What shocked me was that while I had kept quiet about this awful story for over fifty-five years, Wolff had now made it the central theme of his book—and I had had no idea that Wolff was involved in the event in any way.

Near the end of Wolff's book, Abramofsky is killed, and while it is not entirely clear who has shot him, the assumption is that "Mitch Castle," the character in the book who is modeled after Wolff himself, was responsible. My head began to spin. Had Wolff shot Abramofsky in reality? Was it Wolff who had earlier asked Blake to order *me* to do the job? Perhaps I had been wrong about Gates all along! And then I remembered telling Blake that the son of a bitch who ordered this should do it himself. What if Blake actually repeated my words to Wolff and Wolff took them to heart? I began to feel terribly guilty and in some way responsible for the deed. Many a night, I lay awake thinking about it. Finally, I called John Murra, who now lives in upstate New York, to see what he thought of it. He too was shocked to think Wolff could have been ultimately responsible.

In 1997 I spoke with a writer who has conducted in-depth interviews with all the people involved in this incident. He claims to know who executed Abramofsky and is certain it was not Wolff. We may never get to the bottom of this grisly and disturbing mystery, and frankly, for my own peace of mind, I would just as soon never know.

11. THE EBRO OFFENSIVE

1. In later years he was to become a psychiatrist.

2. In 1995 I learned that Royce was still alive. I wrote to his last known address and was both delighted and saddened by his reply. "Dear Harry, Thank you for your letter. I often think of the Spanish war and it still depresses me. The horror of Jarama and the other battles still

are vivid in my mind. I am sorry that I do not remember you or your sister. The only name I remember is Robert (Bob) Merriman who disappeared in the Battle of the Ebro. He was a friend. I hope you have found some happiness in life. That's all there is—there isn't any more."

3. According to many recent visitors to the site, human bones are still strewn across the area.

12. HOME

1. When I left John to go home, he was under the impression that he would never walk again. Fortunately, a wonderful Latvian nurse pressured him to get out of bed and on his feet. Slowly but surely he began to walk, though with a noticeable limp that he still has today.

The fascists were closing in on Barcelona, and the hospital John was in had to release all patients who could manage on their own. Although John was still not fully recuperated, he volunteered with other Internationals to hold back the fascists while wounded soldiers and civilians tried to make their escape to France.

Some time later, John joined up with a group of Americans who were having trouble crossing the French border because they lacked proper papers. One night, they gathered around a single candle in an abandoned hut outside Portbou on the Spanish side of the border. Suddenly, in walked Andre Marty, the top political leader of the International Brigades. He was irate and bellowed at them in French that he would have them shot for having a visible candle lit in the hut. He asked what their nationality was, and John said they were Americans. Perhaps for this reason, he let them go. Eventually, John did get into France, but he spent a difficult three months in a concentration camp at Argeles-sur-Mer and another two months in Le Havre before finally being able to head home.

EPILOGUE

1. I understood immediately. The battle at Teruel took place during a blizzard when the temperature was 20 degrees below zero Fahrenheit. Many soldiers lost toes and fingers from frostbite as a result.

Suggestions for Further Reading

Bessie, Alvah. *Men in Battle*. San Francisco: Chandler and Sharp, 1975.

Bessie, Alvah, and Albert Prago, eds. *Our Fight: Writings by Veterans of the Abraham Lincoln Brigade, Spain 1936–1939*. New York: Monthly Review Press, 1987.

Bowers, Claude. *My Mission to Spain: Watching the Rehearsal for World War II*. New York: Simon and Schuster, 1954.

Brome, Vincent. *The International Brigades: Spain, 1936–1939*. New York: William Morrow, 1966.

Carroll, Peter. *The Odyssey of the Abraham Lincoln Brigade*. Stanford CA: Stanford University Press, 1994.

Colodny, Robert G. *The Struggle for Madrid: The Central Epic of the Spanish Conflict*. New York: Paine-Whitman, 1958.

Del Vayo, Julio Alvarez. *Freedom's Battle*. New York: Hill and Wang, 1971.

Felsen, Milt. *The Anti-Warrior: A Memoir*. Iowa City: University of Iowa Press, 1989.

Geiser, Carl. *Prisoners of the Good Fight*. Westport CT: Lawrence Hill, 1986.

Gerassi, John. *Premature Antifascists: An Oral History*. New York: Praeger, 1986.

Jackson, Gabriel. *The Spanish Republic and the Civil War, 1931–1939*. Princeton: Princeton University Press, 1965.

Katz, William Loren, and Marc Crawford. *The Lincoln Brigade: A Picture History*. New York: Atheneum, 1989.

Kisch, Richard. *They Shall Not Pass: The Spanish People at War, 1936–1939*. London: Wayland, 1974.

Landis, Arthur. *The Abraham Lincoln Brigade*. New York: Citadel, 1967.

Matthews, Herbert. *Half of Spain Died: A Reappraisal of the Spanish Civil War*. New York: Scribner, 1973.

Nelson, Cary, and Jefferson Hendricks. *Collected Poems of Edwin Rolfe*. Urbana and Chicago: University of Illinois Press, 1993.

———. *Madrid 1937: Letters of the Abraham Lincoln Brigade from the Spanish Civil War*. New York: Routledge, 1996.

Nelson, Steve. *The Volunteers*. New York: Mainstream Publishers, 1953.

Payne, Robert. *The Civil War in Spain: 1936–1939*. New York: Putnam, 1962.

Rolfe, Edwin. *The Lincoln Battalion*. New York: Random House, 1939.

Rosenstone, Robert. *Crusade on the Left*. New York: Oxford University Press, 1969.

Sheean, Vincent. *Not Peace but a Sword*. New York: Doubleday, Doran, 1939.

Sperber, Murray A., ed. *And I Remember Spain: A Spanish Civil War Anthology*. New York: Macmillan, 1974.

Thomas, Hugh. *The Spanish Civil War*. New York: Harper, 1961.

Tisa, John. *Recalling the Good Fight: An Autobiography of the Spanish Civil War*. South Hadley MA: Bergen & Garvey, 1985.

Yates, James. *Mississippi to Madrid: Memoirs of a Black American in the Spanish Civil War, 1936–1938*. New York: Shamal, 1986.

Wolff, Milton. *Another Hill*. Urbana and Chicago: University of Illinois Press, 1994.

Index

Abramofsky, Bernard, 140–41, 186
n.11, 187 n.12
Addams, Jane, 4, 5
Aguasvivas, 96
Albacete, 30, 31; as base of operations for Americans, 90, 91, 93,
95, 161; International Brigade
headquarters in, 29; return to, in
1996, 169, 171, 175
Alcorcon, 169–70
All Quiet on the Western Front (Remarque), 39, 56
American Civil Liberties Union
(ACLU), 11
American Commander in Spain
(Merriman and Lerude), 181 n.3
American Legion, 9
Amlie, Hans, 23, 31
Another Hill (Wolff), 187 n.12
Appleton, Owen, 90; death of, 183
ch.8 n.3
Aragon, 77
Armitage, Joseph, 49
Auslander, Dr. Jacob, 182 ch.6 n.1

Bailey, Bill, 14
Barcelona, 77; hospital in, 145, 159–
60, 161, 188 ch.12 n.1; International Brigade headquarters in, 91,
94, 131, 135; leaving Spain from,

162; restaurant in, 132, 186 n.8;
return to, in 1986, 168; return to,
in 1996, 169, 174, 177
Barsky, Dr. Edward, 182 ch.6 n.1
Batea, 119, 127
Berkowitz, Norman, 52, 156; in
Aguasvivas, 96; at Belchite, 80; at
Brunete, 67; during the Ebro Offensive, 147; and Local 1250, xx;
during retreats, 111–12, 121–22,
123, 124, 130, 134, 136, 137, 138;
wounded, 144
Bessie, Alvah, 139, 152, 157, 176
Bianca, Joe, death of, 151, 176
Biegelman, Eli, 51, 52
Bilbao, 85
Blake, Paul, 186 n.11, 187 n.12
Bloom, John Oscar ("Red"), 23, 49–
50
Bottcher, Herman, 28–29, 66, 180
ch.3 n.1
Bradley, Carl, 76–77
Brandt, Joseph, 130, 150
British Battalion, 58, 106, 120, 121,
154, 155, 173, 181 ch.5 n.1, 185
n.5
Brodsky, George, 31
Browder, Earl, 100–101, 183 n.2
Burns, Paul, 44, 60, 61, 62, 75, 155
Byrnes, Joseph, 95–96, 122